DESIGN SENSE

DESIGN SENSE

*A Guide to Getting
the Most from Your
Interior Design Investment*

LINDA BLAIR, ASID

JOHN WILEY & SONS, INC.
New York | Chichester | Brisbane | Toronto | Singapore |

Copyright © 1996 by Linda Blair
Published by John Wiley & Sons, Inc.

Library of Congress Cataloging-in-Publication Data

Blair, Linda, 1939–
    Design sense : a guide to getting the most from your
  interior design investment / Linda Blair.
        p.   cm.
    Includes index.
    ISBN 0-471-14104-6 (cloth : alk. paper)
    1. House furnishings.   2. Interior decoration.   I. Title.
  TX311.B55   1997
  645—dc20   96-12445

Printed in the United States of America

10 9 8 7 6 5 4 3 2 1

I DEDICATE THIS BOOK TO THREE OF THE MOST IMPORTANT PEOPLE IN MY LIFE:

To my mother, Magda Bierman, whose romance with beauty has dominated my personal vision and whose unfailing support has been my anchor.

To my late maternal grandmother, Florence Vogel, who taught me to strive for excellence above all else without losing sight of life's demands and choices.

To my husband, Bill Doescher, a true best friend, who has grown accustomed to my passion for beauty and quality and whose sense of balance, honesty and wisdom helped me survive the arduous task of becoming a writer.

CONTENTS

FOREWORD

*Funeral services for 18th-century elegance were held in the
mid-20th century without fanfare or even any general
cognizance of the occurrence by admirers. Death was
attributed to a variety of causes, including the replacement of
hand labor by machine production and the establishment of
the minimum wage . . . . Most of the friends of elegance were
unaware of the long illness that had preceded its death.*

— from *Quest for the Best*
by Stanley Marcus

WHEN HISTORIANS WRITE about the 1990s, they will call the decade
"The Age of Sloppiness." Clearly, the now generation has lost its sense
of appropriateness. Formality has given way to indifference, which has
deteriorated into negligence.

Do you remember when it was generally accepted protocol to travel
dressed up—men in coats and ties, women in dresses and high heels?
Nowadays, people board airplanes in bikini tops and shabby tie-dyed
shirts, or with their underwear showing.

Happily, the situation isn't necessarily permanent.

If you remember your history, ancient Roman society teemed with excesses. Ultimately, however, the people rejected that way of life. Today we, too, are reevaluating our way of thinking, our social institutions, and our lifestyles. The pendulum is beginning to swing.

Let me say, then, that I am guardedly optimistic that the demand for quality will return. In fact, I see signs of it already. Our free enterprise system continues to provide discretionary income for such pleasures as travel, personal ornamentation, and interior decoration. More and more, spending shows a return to refinement and appreciation of excellence. Mechanization and industrialization have seriously eroded the fine craftsmanship that existed in the seventeenth and eighteenth centuries, yet costs have stabilized so that more people can afford today's luxuries. As I see it, they appear to be availing themselves of those commodities.

Moreover, as I check through leftovers at the end of each buying season—after the markdowns and the sales—I find junk. Junk! The public is buying quality and leaving the junk behind. I am encouraged.

True, the number of purveyors of fine merchandise has dwindled considerably. The reason, I think, is not high prices so much as poor business practices and an unwillingness to adapt. Quality stores largely have neglected to educate their staffs about the advantages of quality merchandise, and they have failed to address the importance of service. Furthermore, they don't understand the public, what the public is buying, and why. Retailers could learn a lesson from their counterparts in mail order, who monitor every single sale.

Elegance, I fear, still lies dormant. Standardization is the byword today. If you were to drop a woman by parachute into a large shopping center anywhere in the United States, probably she wouldn't know where she was.

How refreshing, then, to find a simpatico mentality in Linda Blair, a woman who has dedicated her career to elevating people's ways of thinking by showing them that good quality is the path to good value. In so doing, she is raising the collective standard of living by encouraging people to live more comfortable, more satisfying and, yes, more elegant lives.

This book is her manifesto. Read it. Learn from it. Follow its precepts.

— Stanley Marcus
Founder and president emeritus of the Neiman Marcus stores

PREFACE

I AM FORTUNATE to have been involved with interior design and decorating for much of my life. Over the years, I've learned that this is a demanding business, requiring dedication, creativity, imagination, and problem-solving skills that combine good design and good value.

I'm passionate about meeting the challenges of this exciting field and achieving client satisfaction. My primary reason for writing this book is to enable consumers to further understand the complicated process of interior design and to achieve a clearer understanding of the values inherent in the design process.

Helping people analyze, plan, and organize their lives with accompanying beauty and style defines the framework of good design. Individualizing the end result—making it a personal statement that bespeaks harmony of design and comfort—characterizes my own customer focus.

In this preface, and throughout the book, I will discuss the philosophy, historical concepts, ideas, techniques, and professional design expertise that will help you realize your dreams for a new home under construction or an older one that needs to look and work better.

WHO I AM

My earliest recollection of interiors and design is of myself as a toddler, standing in the middle of my room repositioning my collection of picture books in terms of light source and determining the best placement for stuffed animals in relation to dolls and accessories for quick access from both the sleeping and the playing areas. A precocious child?

Not really. Just in touch early on with a designer's eye, language, thinking, scrutiny, and point of view—virtually from the womb.

"Designer genes," says one of my staff members. Perhaps so, considering that I am a third-generation interior designer, who followed my mother and grandmother into the field. By predetermination, then, as well as by training and experience, I am indeed an interior designer, believing firmly that good design is a worthwhile pursuit that rewards its followers with more organized, more serene, and more productive lives.

A designer studies the past to arrive at the present. Just as a writer needs to understand the discipline of grammar rules before taking creative risks in expression, a designer studies classical principles in order to create new and satisfying schemes.

Designers are observant. They see what others pass by or simply take for granted. And they remember—combining bits and pieces of thoughtful intelligence into functional and attractive design plans that solve space problems.

DESIGN AS A DECISION-MAKING TOOL

Design has influenced decision making for most of my life — through my childhood and teenage years, college, graduate school and design school, as a wife and mother, as a businesswoman.

- How to arrange my childhood bedroom to coincide with my moods or the seasons of the year.

- How to set up my apartment for maximum efficiency to establish good study habits and accomplish tasks expediently.

- How to reconcile my lovingly amassed collections of antique tabletop accessories with my husband's obsession with sports memorabilia.

- How to set up our home to accommodate my predilection for memento-filled environments with his modern, clean-lines mindset.

- How to make logistical sense out of the comings and goings of four active children.

- How to turn 1,500 square feet of office space into a professional suite that will illustrate design options for clients without overwhelming them, and to motivate an office staff of creative individuals without inhibiting their own sense of style.

A good designer is a problem solver. I wake up every day eager to get started—to seek design solutions for my clients, to teach design techniques to my students, and to show people how to improve their quality of life by applying basic design principles like balance and proportion.

I love sizing things up or down so that furniture and accessories fit into the space conveniently and artistically. I also need to know who's coming and going or how people get from one room to another. To provide good design and good value, a designer considers questions such as who's using the space and who's just passing through, and what activities will take place in that space today and later on.

Good design information provides the means for you to get the most out of your living environment. With good information, you can own the solutions. Helping you find those solutions is what I'm all about.

A BOOK FOR THE NOVICE OR EXPERIENCED PLANNER

Since you have purchased this book, I trust you agree with me that good design is worth pursuing. Perhaps you are a design novice, moving into your first home and anxious about making mistakes that can be costly in the long run. Your concern is well founded.

Let's say you want to buy carpeting. You choose a thick pile that's the most expensive—ergo, you reason, the best quality. Not a good choice if you intend to put it in a dining room where chairs should move in and out easily without getting hung up in a deep plush. Yes, buy top quality, but buy a tightly woven low pile that facilitates movement and that furniture will sit up on, not sink into.

Here's another example, and a common misconception: buy cheaply made, less expensive juvenile furniture because children grow up so quickly. This is very shortsighted.

First, children's furniture takes a beating; jumping and leaping and bouncing seem to go hand in hand with growing up. Fiberboard may be cost effective (for adult as well as children's furnishings), but it won't go the distance.

And second, well-made pieces—baby rocking chairs and small chests particularly, even those scarred with the patina of youth—make charming accent pieces later on when used elsewhere in the house.

Let's look at a child's room from another angle. Perhaps you're a young married, planning a family later. You might naturally want to make the spare bedroom a den first and later the baby's room. Smart buying can serve both purposes, giving you a sleek, upbeat den now, a stylishly perky room for baby when it's time.

On the other hand, you may be quite practiced at pulling rooms together, and you may have considerable experience in planning and executing interior spaces. From time to time, you may have worked with an interior design professional and may know a great deal about choosing new paint, wallpaper, and fabric.

But good design is more than that. I can show you how to analyze a room in terms of its use and how to plan space for workable answers that respond to function and aesthetics—not only right now, but into the future. Good design is a lasting and economically sound solution.

DEVELOP YOUR OWN STYLE

Learn to see with a designer's eye. Keep a scrapbook filled with ideas you've gleaned from places you've visited and products and materials you like. As you begin to see a style emerge—shapes, wood types, finishes, textiles, colors—you will begin to develop confidence in your own judgment and ability to put materials together in a pleasing and tasteful way.

Resist trends. Trust your instincts. Good design is good design whether or not it reflects a particular style that happens to be in vogue.

You may remember when, a few years ago, everybody wanted a "Southwestern room." If I had a nickel for every can of Southwestern sand-tone beige paint or one of its hundred derivatives sold during that period, well . . . .

The point is, just because a particular style is hot, it doesn't necessarily follow that a room done in that style is good design. It's not the trend that makes the room; success depends on how well the room is conceived, planned, and executed. In terms of Southwestern, some are good; many aren't. Some truly fine Southwestern rooms have endured because they are true and authentic; others appear stilted and disingenuous.

FOCUS IS KEY TO DESIGN SUCCESS

Let's look at something classic. I've seen, for instance, excellent period rooms filled with valuable antiques. I've also seen antique-filled rooms that are overdone, heavy, and ponderous.

You like modern, you say— clean lines, stark, a few carefully placed objects, no color contrast. Yes, a good look . . . especially when there's a focus. Good contemporary rooms look deceptively simple but, in fact, are deceivingly substantive.

Every room, of any period, any style, or any agenda, needs focus to direct the eye and anchor the space. And every room needs warmth, a single personality-revealing piece or small collection of items (related or not) that define the people who live there. *Feng shui* masters, purveyors of the ancient Oriental philosophy based on the harmonious placement of man-made structures in space, call this the wealth corner—a gorgeous concept, I think.

AN ANCIENT PHILOSOPHY
WITH MODERN APPLICATIONS

The wealth corner is one of the most intriguing *feng shui* concepts—a strong focal point, a positioning of powerful and important items or resources of value to the household in full view. Similarly, good decorating calls for focal points that set off a room with visual interest.

You can create a wealth corner by first determining who you are and what you want to accomplish. Then furnish it with symbols that will help you achieve your goals.

For instance, I placed a mockup of this book prominently in my own wealth corner. The finished product that you hold suggests there may be more to *feng shui* than Far Eastern mystery.

While participating in a presentation on the craft of *feng shui,* I learned that the ancient principles adapt well to modern concepts of interior design. Good design begins with a good plan, and a good plan begins with a candid analysis of who you are, who's using the room, and how the room should function, now and later. Like *feng shui*, good design addresses the personality of space, its architecture, and the ebb and flow of natural light and energy.

I CARE ABOUT YOU

As a professional designer I care about you and how you live. I care about your comfort—how you sit, how you sleep, whether you have the proper light to read by. I care about your family and your guests, whether you like to throw big parties, entertain at intimate dinner parties, invite the gang in for the Super Bowl, or have the kids over for pizza after the game.

I care about your children and what they do for fun. I want to know the games they play, their favorite toys, how they like school.

I want to know about your habits, your likes, your dreams, your vision. Are you a hunter and gatherer, a collector, a pack rat? Are you dedicated to the practical—music on the piano, not framed on an end table; maps bound into an atlas on the bookshelf, not hanging on a wall? Does your kitchen display every copper pot in your repertoire? Or do you revel in antiseptic white with nary a crumb, much less a toaster, to violate pristine countertops?

At the end of our design journey, you will have the raw materials and new insights to help you make intelligent design decisions that will suit you and serve your life-style. You will know that a successful room not only is aesthetically pleasing and functional, but also needs to call out, to speak. And perhaps most essential, you will know when and why you must seek professional help from a trained interior designer.

In any case, you will forevermore look at your home differently, more intuitively and with greater understanding of how it can be put together, and how its design can affect all phases of your life.

YOUR ADVOCATE

Some years ago, two consumer advocates won the trust of Americans with a realistic, good-for-the-consumer approach. Ralph Nader took on the big guys and called foul when they took advantage of us by charging too much for inferior goods. Betty Furness opened refrigerator doors in television commercials, but we believed what she told us about features that would make our lives easier.

As the self-appointed dean of the Good Value School of Design, I've devoted my career to teaching consumers how to make good design and buying decisions. With the passionate zeal of a Ralph Nader and the pragmatic approach of a Betty Furness, I will—in the words and pictures that follow—empower you to make sound design choices, to analyze, plan, and organize so that you will enjoy lives of harmony, beauty, and comfort.

Linda Blair, ASID

ACKNOWLEDGMENTS

None of us really does anything alone. And surely the creation of this book never could have been possible without the spirit, skills, and stamina of Sara Bloom. Her unrivaled talent, patience and persistence were responsible for the completion of the writing process.

Thanks also to Joanne Schreiber and Rose Bennett Gilbert for their advice and encouragement. Special appreciation to Michelle Blair, Marianne McNulty, Tracy Holmes, Siobhan Carroll, Pat Hamilton, and Gail Resen for their help and support.

And my deep gratitude to Stanley Marcus, founder and president emeritus of the Neiman Marcus stores, for providing a foreword that only a man of his devotion to good design and value could have written.

Linda Blair

1
MAKE A PLAN

Good design doesn't just happen, it is carefully planned. A good plan considers scope, proportion, activities, use, style, traffic patterns, personality, aesthetic preferences, and budget. With a good design plan, space responds to immediate as well as future needs.

—RITA CARSON GUEST, ASID, ATLANTA

You Don't Have to Put the Phones Where the Phone Jacks Are

SUCCESSFUL DESIGN BEGINS with a plan. Rooms that work don't happen willy-nilly. You've got to grab a room by the collar and lay down the law.

You can freshen a room with paint or give it a lift with new curtains, but without a plan you'll be cheating yourself, denying yourself the unique possibilities that each room offers.

You own the space, after all, and probably pay dearly in rent, mortgage, or maintenance fees, not to mention real estate taxes, to call it your own. Make it work for you. Let it serve your needs. Don't just dress it up, whip it into shape. With a good plan, you own the solution.

A case in point: You don't have to put the phones where the phone jacks are, or the TV where the antenna is, or the pictures where the hooks are. If you find this an enlightening concept, then you're about to have your design consciousness raised. Open your mind to possibilities, take nothing for granted, and look at the big picture.

DON'T SQUEEZE IN, DESIGN IN

The whole is greater than the sum of its parts. The smallest detail contributes to this whole—the room in question—and should be carefully planned, thoughtfully designed in.

What do I mean by designed in? Let's say an art director designs a brochure for a client. Every element has been carefully considered and chosen to create a unified whole. A point of view has been determined, the copy written and approved; the size of the type, type style, line leading, paper stock, and ink color selected. It's a strong piece, eye-catching and persuasive. At the last minute, the client says, "I thought of something else I want to say. You can squeeze it in someplace, right?"

This is the moment the art director takes the poison pill. Yes, you can squeeze it in someplace, but it will forever look squeezed in, out of proportion to other copy, photos, and graphic elements. You don't want this to happen to your room.

Interior design, like graphic design, considers all the elements—colors, fabrics, traffic patterns, furniture placement, light sources, storage, ventilation, sound quality, entrances and exits, activities, ambiance, overall statement, proportion and, yes, telephones. To consider any of the elements unimportant to the whole is a mistake. Sooner or later, that "unimportant" element will mar the effect, will become a wart and a wrinkle you will forever be trying to hide.

Plan in advance for all contingencies. And plan on replanning—rethinking—as your life takes new turns.

CONSIDER EVERY ELEMENT

The height of the windows, the size of the furnishings, and the color of the walls and ceilings are as important as the depth and placement of the moldings, the height of the artwork you hang on the walls, and even where you put your telephone.

Just because a telephone installer arbitrarily chose an easy access spot for the telephone jack is no reason that you can't have your telephone on the opposite wall. The installer never considered your lifestyle, whether you're right- or left-handed, how you intend to group furniture, what activities will take place in your room, the style of your furniture, and whether you intend to sit at a desk while using the telephone or ease into a chair up close to a window so you can talk while keeping an eye on the bird feeder. Why not? It's relaxing and refreshing, and it's your prerogative to do so if it pleases you.

Those who say "don't worry about details" don't understand interior design. When designers consider a room, they see the total scheme, and they also see every individual element, every minute detail that goes into it. To a designer, every detail counts.

ATTENTION TO DESIGN MEANS YOU CARE

Wherever my husband and I go—to a meeting, out to dinner, in and out of hotels and buildings and tourist sights—I'm always pointing out design flaws and architectural mistakes. And Bill says, "Who cares?" The answer is, I care. I truly do.

And when it comes to your own home, you should care, too. Take a good hard look, and tell the truth. Are you seeing rooms that don't work, that inconvenience you and your family and guests, that are dark and depressing? You don't have to live this way. These rooms can be made to function better, to fulfill your needs, to lift your spirits. An investment in your home will reap dividends for many years to come. Good design delivers long-lasting value.

A woman I know moved into a charming older home—nine rooms, good floor plan, plenty of natural light (unusual in older homes), a small but workable kitchen, and an expandable attic to accommodate future needs. Upstairs, four bedrooms, two baths; downstairs, the usual three, plus den and maid's bedroom/bathroom suite off the back entrance. Sounds ideal. It could have been.

The woman never intended to use the maid's quarters for a maid. Once-a-week household help was all she ever needed or could afford. She turned the maid's room into an office and made the bathroom the downstairs powder room. So far, so good. Except the bathroom was a *full* bath—complete with large tub. And this tub, as it turned out, caused problems from the moment the moving van pulled away from the curb.

PARDON ME, YOUR TUB IS SHOWING

Occupying more than half the square footage of the bathroom, the tub prevents people from stepping back to see themselves properly in the mirror over the sink, and it crowds the commode. The bathtub is simply too large and ungainly for the size of the room, undistinguished in design (no claw feet for period interest, no unusual shape) and gets in the way of any attempts to upgrade the look of the room. It doesn't even lend itself to hanging an interesting piece of art on the wall.

Others might have removed the tub, but not my friend.

"When I go to sell the house, three full bathrooms will be more valuable to a prospective buyer than two and a half," she observes.

Maybe so. But to preserve the value of a three-full-bath house, my friend, her family, and her guests have sacrificed convenience and aesthetics by tripping over an ugly tub for more than 26 years. By removing the tub, she could have turned a cumbersome full bath into a charming powder room that retained the vintage look while providing modern conveniences. The investment would repay her fivefold were she to sell the house today.

GOOD INTENTIONS GONE AWRY

At the other extreme, a Long Island weekly newspaper recently carried a story by a clever writer poking fun at herself for redecorating her guest room because of a book of poems given to her by a friend.

To match the rich green cover of the small volume, she repainted the walls, replaced the bedspread, curtains, and carpeting, and purchased a small antique night table to hold the new lamp and the book.

Maybe the room needed an aesthetic upgrade, anyway. But maybe, as long as she was willing to invest the time and the money in raw materials, she should have started with a more thoughtful room plan— one that would have made the space appear larger (or smaller, as the case may be) and brighter and airier. She might have considered ambient lighting to set an overall mood suggestive of the poetry and built in serviceable task lighting conducive to reading verse. A good designer would have told the writer not to even consider color until the space was planned, not to do lighting until the furniture layout was complete.

A thoughtful room plan would have delivered a magical place for the writer to treasure all her life. Good design would have produced better value, although probably not as engaging a story.

PLAN THE WORK; WORK THE PLAN

You may have ideas about how you want your room to look. Until you transfer those ideas to paper, you won't know if everything is going to fit or how it all will fit together.

A plan is a clear definition of scope, proportion, activities, use, traffic pattern, style, personality and aesthetic preferences, and budget. It defines a use of space, spells out location, and coordinates furnishings and accessories.

Consider scope and proportion first. Good design techniques can make a room appear more elegant and gracious than its actual bare-bones structure would suggest. Take into account the cards you are dealt, and then plan how you will play the hand for best effect. For best results, consider the following ideas:

❖ *What useful purpose does the room serve?* Some rooms provide a simple answer: a family room, a bedroom. That's now. But what about later?

Prepare a future needs assessment. Will the bedroom become an exercise room once the children are grown? Will the family room become a home office? Plan ahead with plenty of electrical outlets (you can never have too many!) and built-ins to accommodate all activities: storage and easy access for kids' toys now, or cords and phones and computer components later. Maximize your investment by planning now for the future.

❖ *Who will use the room?* Is it a hideaway for dad or a place for the neighborhood hockey team to congregate, complete with youthful exuberance, plenty of snacks, the usual horsing around, and piles of hockey equipment?

Worst case scenario: the hockey team. Okay. How do all the players get into the room? Do they charge through the front door, sweep through the living room, and leave a trail of destruction in their wake? If that's the case, rethink the living room furniture arrangement, and consider a durable floor covering.

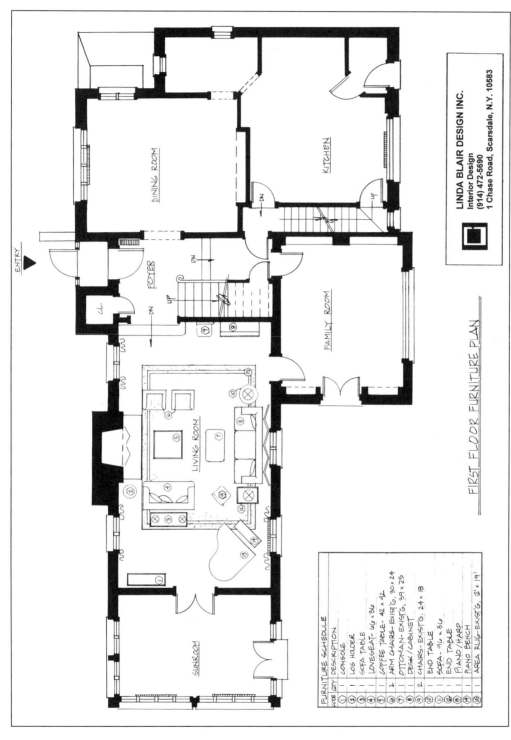

FURNITURE SCHEDULE

CODE	QTY	DESCRIPTION
1	1	CONSOLE
2	1	LOG HOLDER
3	1	SOFA TABLE
4	1	LOVESEAT- 60 × 36
5	1	COFFEE TABLE- 42 × 42
6	2	ARM CHAIRS- EXIST'G, 30 × 24
7	1	OTTOMAN- EXIST'G, 39 × 25
8	1	DESK / CABINET
9	2	CHAIRS- EXIST'G, 24 × 18
10	1	END TABLE
11	1	SOFA- 96 × 36
12	1	END TABLE
13	1	PIANO/HARP
14	1	PIANO BENCH
15	1	AREA RUG-EXIST'G, 12' × 19'

FIRST FLOOR FURNITURE PLAN

ENTRY

FOYER

DINING ROOM

KITCHEN

FAMILY ROOM

LIVING ROOM

SUNROOM

LINDA BLAIR DESIGN INC.
Interior Design
(914) 472-5690
1 Chase Road, Scarsdale, N.Y. 10583

The 16-foot-wide by 28-foot-long size of this living room may seem adequate, but allowing for necessary traffic patterns leaves limited room for furnishings.

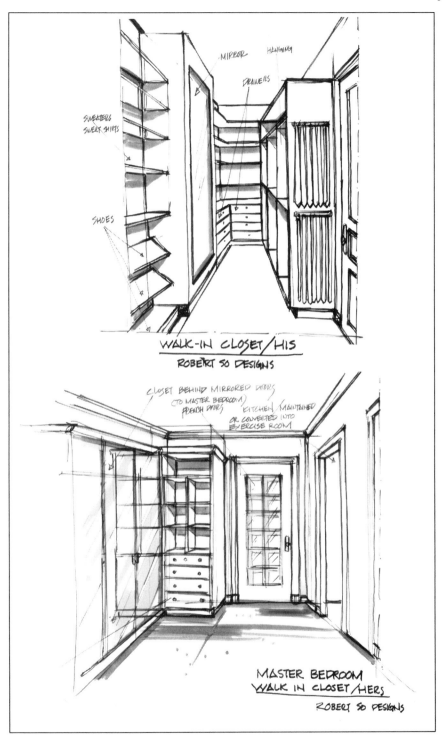

WALK-IN CLOSET/HIS
ROBERT SO DESIGNS

MASTER BEDROOM
WALK IN CLOSET/HERS
ROBERT SO DESIGNS

Closets planned to organize possessions reflect skillful design and provide one of life's most basic creature comforts.

Credits: interior designer and renderer Robert So, Allied Member ASID

Maybe there's a better way. How about redirecting traffic through a back entrance? Doesn't work, you say? Remember the phone jacks. Can it be made to work? Can you create a hallway or a mud room with some built-in storage for outerwear and equipment and a take-a-beating, easy-cleanup floor?

Let's take another example. Suppose you decide you want to freshen up a den with new curtains. Nice. Are you going to run out to the fabric store and choose a pattern? Or are you going to think about how the room is used and what new curtains can accomplish, and whether another type of window covering may be more appropriate?

Do you need to darken a room somewhat for an afternoon nap? Completely darken for showing slides? Should you consider window coverings that can also perform as insulators that keep cold out and warmth in? For maximum benefit and value from your purchase, you need to consider how the room is used before you decide what to buy.

❖ *Function is not all, certainly.* Taste, judgment, and personal preference make a space yours. A room should reflect your personality; feature colors that flatter you; make you feel comfortable, relaxed, and stress-free; and introduce patterns that cheer you, not make your room feel busy.

❖ *Planning includes budget as well as space.* The financial approach may be of the sky's-the-limit variety or, like most people's, a sensible assessment of needs without unreasonable stress on the bank account. In either case, success depends on how well you plan and how well you execute your plan. Unless carefully thought out, a simple facelift is as wasteful as a complex renovation.

Like a good coat, a room has to wear well. You want to be as happy and comfortable in it a few years hence as you are on the first outing. You want your coat—and your room—to look attractive season after season, to feel that the cost was worthwhile.

A good basic Blairstyle rule is to invest in one top-notch piece of furniture rather than a lot of inferior pieces that will fill up a room quickly. If you buy a good sofa—one that supports your body properly—you can recover it two or three times in its lifetime and know that you have a quality piece that always will look attractive and provide proper health benefits.

On the other hand, suppose you find a bargain bookcase. It's the right size and color and will get all those books out of the boxes, up off the floor and in place that very afternoon. You run the risk, though, that those quickie shelves will soon show more sag than an aging dowager. She may be able to beat a hasty retreat to her plastic surgeon, but nothing can help those bookshelves—except new shelving.

Remember, there's bargain furniture and there's quality furniture. Watch out for bargain-quality furniture!

Designing begins in the mind; here the preliminary shapes and forms of the furniture start to emerge as the room's landscape. See color insert page 5 for finished room.

Credit: interior designer Linda Blair, ASID; renderer Robert So

GET STARTED

To get your plan under way, take out your tape measure, and plot your room on graph paper, using ¼ inch = 1 foot as a standard. Mark off the entrances, doors, windows, and architectural details. Pick up a scaled furniture chart (most furniture stores have them), cut out your chairs and tables, and arrange them on the graph. Draw arrows to indicate traffic patterns, allowing 2- to 3-foot-wide passages. When your room is down on paper, it will look very different, and possibilities will emerge.

You may think of your room as square when in reality it's rectangular; it may feel square because of furniture groupings. You may think the room is small, but its actual dimensions may prove otherwise; it may seem small because the elements are out of proportion.

Only after studying the space on paper did one homeowner see that by removing the wall that separated the kitchen from the laundry room behind she could create a breakfast nook. The discovery—and a relatively small investment—created an eat-in kitchen that considerably upgraded the aesthetics as well as the market value of her house.

Think through what you need and what you are trying to accomplish. Factor in who you are. Don't plan space to please your friends, satisfy your mother, or honor Aunt Estelle, who thought artwork in the bathroom was superfluous. This is your room. Plan it well, and it will forever be a valued addition to your life.

ONE STEP AT A TIME

Remember, you don't have to implement your entire plan at once. Take it step by step: structural changes, carpentry, room colors, window dressing, lighting, floor covering, furniture, accessories. Buy good quality that will serve well through the years, one piece at a time if that's what's comfortable for you.

The wonderful part about a good plan—and good design—is that if it's good, it can wait. Good design is as good tomorrow as it is today, next month, next year, and when you finish the project. Unfettered by the vagaries of fashion and trend, good design endures.

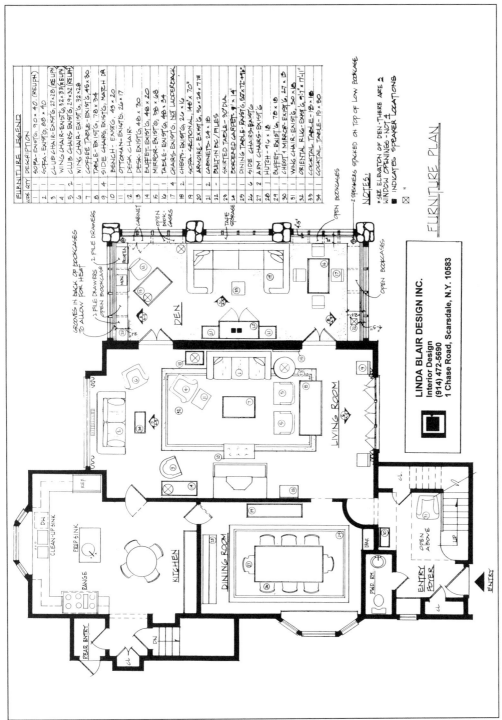

Creating a plan for the whole house or apartment offers a bird's eye view of the entire space at one glance, permits coordination throughout all spaces, and provides an excellent opportunity to assess existing and new furnishings in advance.

Credits: interior designer Linda Blair, ASID

Even in a bedroom, designing a plan is essential to make certain that basics, such as adequate storage, good lighting, and a reading chair, are present whenever possible.

Credits: interior designer and renderer Robert So, Allied Member ASID

*B*lairstyle Tips *for Making a Space Your Own*

❖ THE PERSONALITY PREFERENCES PROFILE TEST

Here's a little test to determine how design elements can mirror personality. Answer yes or no to the following 10 questions. Be honest.

1. My basic wardrobe piece is a navy blazer with brass buttons.
2. I like to plan my weekends.
3. I always wear shoes, even in the house.
4. Television bores me.
5. I can't leave the house until the breakfast dishes are done.
6. I'm a morning person.
7. I love to entertain.
8. I love to be entertained.
9. The invention of the fax machine is the best news of the decade.
10. My dining room table is rectangular.

Score 10 points for each yes answer.

❖ If you scored 90 to 100, you are ultra-pragmatic, into no-nonsense colors, uncluttered lines, and simple pattern. White and subtle beige broken up with stripes and herringbone tweed are good choices for you. Build in plenty of attic and basement storage to keep living space uncluttered. Locate the family room as far from the living and dining rooms as possible. Illuminate with track lighting. Look for a single absolutely outstanding antique piece for each room in your house. Invest in a desk for yourself that is off-limits to the rest of the family. Hang large-format art.

❖ If you scored 70 to 90 points, you're purposeful with a fun-loving streak. You'll find neutral colors with large floral prints and plaids appealing. A big kitchen that opens into a family room with a fireplace is a good bet for you. Ceiling borders and chair-railing moldings will appeal. Large windows that flood rooms with lots of natural light will bring the outside in. Country and rustic are good styles for you. An Oriental rug will add design interest and a soft edge to linear wood and upholstered pieces.

❖ A score of 40 to 60 points indicates a soft nature that will respond well to pastels, small prints, and lots of surface area to display souvenirs, collectibles, and cherished mementos. Plan big closets with lots of shelving for quick access to possessions, and area rugs with colorful geometric patterns to define furniture groupings. Install a mobile in the living room.

❖ Under 40 points, you are an incurable romantic, utterly spontaneous. Experiment with unusual colors and soft prints in unexpected places. Be bold in the living room, demure in the dining room, fanciful in the kitchen, seductive in the bedroom. Shades of green, splashed with yellow are good colors. Plants thrive under your care, and flowers cheer you. Build yourself a fabulous bathroom. Display lots of photos.

2
WALLS
AND
CEILINGS

*I see backgrounds in much the
same way a painter sees a blank
canvas or an actor an empty stage.
The background of a room sets the
mood and, as such, should reflect
the activities that will take place
there, and enhance the interaction
of the people within.*
—GARY E. WHEELER, FASID
MINNEAPOLIS

Walls—Bend Them to Your Will

GOOD DESIGN BEGINS with walls.

Four walls—so accepting of the simplest design solution and so
equally accommodating of the most complex.

Four walls—a joyful opportunity to array and enliven a room? Or
an overwhelming, echoing expanse of emptiness?

Four walls—understandably intimidating. Take a typical 12-foot-
square room, the size of an average den or guest bedroom. With 8-foot
ceilings, you have 384 square feet of wall space, minus windows and
doorways, to handle. That's nearly three times the floor space.

The marvelous thing about walls *is* their size. As a room element,
their vastness powerfully influences space. Make your walls feel special.
Enhance them with color, paint finishes, wall hangings, and art.

Sometimes four walls aren't enough. You can make walls within walls—using screens, glass-block projections, bookcases, and highback furniture—to add architectural interest and verticality, to define activity centers, or to introduce color groupings.

And don't think it obligatory to line your furniture flat against the walls. Float some pieces in the space, angling away from the walls, to create L-shapes and other unexpected forms.

Keep in mind that good design can push out walls or make them seem cozy and comforting—without lifting a hammer. Walls present exciting challenges, indeed.

AN AFFORDABLE FIX

The easiest treatment for walls—and often the most effective—is to paint them. A few gallons of the best-quality paint (in relative as well as absolute terms, paint is inexpensive enough always to insist on the absolute best) can make space feel wonderful. For less than $100 and careful preparation underneath, you can roll on a wonderfully smooth, almost velvety wall covering that sets a luxurious tone and animates furnishings and accessories.

For good value, good quality is the key. Inferior brands go on thin and stringy. Quality paint is thick and rich, like cream, with sensuous colors that envelop or vivid brights that set up boldly, calling out for attention. Paint is a quick fix. And lasting. With proper preparation—sanding and priming—a good paint job can last as long as five years.

Even in a rental apartment, when management offers to decorate your unit, it's worth the added expense to provide your own paint. You *can* do that, you know. And you'll be so much happier with the results. Whether you own or rent, house-sit or bunk in, it's your home and it should be worthy of you. When walls need a new coat, nothing less than cashmere will do.

Special finishing techniques, like glazing (for a polyurethane effect), dragging or combing (brushing texture into wet paint), and ragging or sponging (dabbing on texture) are long-lasting effects, but best left to the experts. An amateur job will create rather than camouflage flaws.

As an example, consider my elephant man. This gentleman had gone to great lengths to paint two living room walls an elephant gray color, which he then sponged lightly with pink and blue to obtain a mottled effect. Actually, what he achieved was more of a motley effect.

Nevertheless, he had chosen the colors himself, and had erected a scaffold to "do the job right," he said, gazing up admiringly at his handiwork. Over time, with family members and guests equally under-whelmed with the color scheme, I persuaded him to let a professional painter sponge the walls a soft, creamy neutral. The result? At last, a unified, dignified space.

INVENTIVE COLOR CHOICE

Let's look at some prime (no pun intended) examples of paint color choices. A young couple shopping for their first house found exactly what they were looking for—an older home with a stone fireplace, mahogany woodwork, graceful archways that introduced the living and dining rooms from the center hall, and stucco walls throughout.

Here was rustic, old-world charm with built-in childproofing: dark woodwork to mask scuff marks and textured walls to hide fingerprints. A fresh coat of paint, and the moving van could begin unloading.

Savvy about the properties of white, they carefully shopped the various hues and decided that soft eggshell would bring out the warmth of the mahogany throughout the house . . . except for the dining room, that is, which they intended to keep as an adults-only (mostly, anyway) sanctuary. And, frankly, that suited the youngsters just fine. They were much happier eating in the kitchen, where sticky fingers and spilled milk wouldn't sully hallowed ground.

To define the space as their own, the couple sought to separate it from the rest of the house and, at the same time, reflect their own personality and taste. A vibrant twosome, their recipe for an enjoyable evening was a dinner party combining equal parts interesting people and unusual foods. In choosing a color to dine by, the new homeowners were looking for one that would keep the conversation upbeat, complement food, and, finally, set this room apart. They chose red.

Red stimulates the appetite and makes spirits soar. Red is a magnifi-cent dining room surround.

AN IMAGINATIVE SOLUTION

Then there's Charlie—a youngster with imagination, style and an indulgent family. A few years ago, when Charlie was just seven, he announced to his parents that he wanted to redo his room. His idea was to bring the outside in.

Lots of kids bring the outside in. They get mud in their sneakers, grass in their hair, and dirt under their fingernails. They fill their pockets with rocks, wood chips, onion grass, bottle caps, and the occasional frog.

Charlie figured that he was happiest when he was outdoors—playing in the sunshine, skimming rocks over the pond, and camping out, crawling out of his tent at night to peer up at the stars. It just didn't seem right to him to give all that up in the one place where he spent most of his time—his room.

Charlie visualized the closets flanking his desk alcove as trees, their branches and leaves reaching up to the ceiling, which he planned to decorate as sky with large, fluffy white clouds. The east window would become the morning sun, its painted rays poking out of the window frame and onto the walls. The west wall, nurtured in Charlie's vision by the warmth of the sun, would contain the lake with a rainbow above.

He would paint the baseboard to resemble blades of grass growing up out of his green rug, and speckle his door in shades of blue to create the illusion of walking through a waterfall.

Charlie, along with his mom, dad, and sister, brought off the earthly treasures—trees, sky, lake, waterfall, rainbow, and sunshine—with paint, rollers, brushes, and a few sponges for dabbing on leaves and grass.

Clearly, Charlie's concept is not for everyone. Nor is a red dining room. Yet there's a lesson to be learned. You need to think about how you live, what happens in the room, what message you want to convey, and what makes you happy.

WALLCOVERING OPTIONS

Wallcoverings—paper, fabric, wood, tile, et al.—can add pattern and texture to walls, creating many different effects. It's important to choose the right one for the space.

❖ *Vinyls and papers* are available in every imaginable style. Even the most subtle colors and patterns vocalize; good design ensures that they'll speak clearly.

On the whole, strippable, scrubbable vinyls bring color, pattern, and easy maintenance to kitchens and children's rooms. Background papers in subtle prints or solids add a softening element to bedrooms and formal rooms. Totally out of date now are foil papers and flocked prints. And never use paper in a bathroom with a shower. Steam loosens even the best fixatives and pulls the paper from the wall.

I use very little paper, and then only for background. Pattern repeats tend to jump, drawing the eye to the walls instead of to something wonderful on the walls, like a piece of art or a fine collection of antique plates.

Paper borders, on the other hand, add definition to a room. Use them on the ceiling, at the ceiling line, as a chair rail, at the baseboard, or up and around doors and windows. You can use borders with papered or painted walls.

❖ *Fabrics* make good wallcoverings, providing a splendid way to hide less-than-perfect walls, while capitalizing on visual appeal. Here is an opportunity to introduce elements of softness and surprise—to inject individuality—by considering a wall covering not designed specifically for walls.

In choosing fabric, stick with a tight weave; loose weaves tend to stretch. Sheer fabrics work best in small areas if shirred or box pleated.

To attach fabric, nail or staple it directly onto the walls, or preserve the wall finish by putting up narrow, lightweight furring strips. Attach strips along the ceiling line and at the baseboard with half-inch nails, and tack the fabric to the wood. Pull tight without stretching. If you choose a pattern, be sure the fabric is attached and pulled straight; wavy lines are distracting and indicate an amateur at work. For best results, hire a professional installer.

❖ *Aged wood* produces the ultimate country kitchen, den, or family room. If you're lucky enough to hear about a cache of antique floor boards or other antique wood, rush to the site. Good aged wood is hard to come by; if you really want it, and you can find it, pay whatever you must. Alternatively, look for woodworkers or shops that specialize in furniture made from used wood. Recycled wood creates an "it's always been there" atmosphere.

Caveat: Be sure used wood is treated for insects before installation, and then never worry about it again.

❖ *Wood paneling*, a popular wall treatment of the past, cannot compare to authentic boards, even if the paneling is made of hardwood veneers. If you cover your walls with paneling instead of real boards, you will lose the feel, texture, and pattern of wood. When installing cabinetry, add wood fascia to blank walls for wrap-around warmth and the unbeatable patina of aged wood.

Imitation wood paneling in vinyl or paper is yet a poorer choice: costly, fragile, and totally fake. A bad investment.

❖ *Wainscoting*, less rustic than barn boards and highly decorative, is created from natural wood boards built by a cabinetmaker and installed vertically, usually below a chair rail. Depending on the wood, you can leave wainscoting natural or paint it. The result is always handsome, simple, and a highly effective way to add hand-finished wood to walls.

❖ *Chair railings* are strips of molding that run around the perimeter of the room at approximately chair-back height. I like to think of a chair rail as a belt that finishes off a look—an accessory that ties a well-dressed room together. You can use various styles of molding for a chair rail. With wainscoting below, a simple wallpaper or velvety paint above, and perhaps a dramatic border accent, your room begins to glow.

❖ *Mirrors* as wall decor provide depth that simply isn't there. They can augment the presumed space and also play interesting tricks with light, bouncing it onto ceiling and walls or reflecting it back into a room to brighten and surprise.

Use mirrors sparingly. Whole walls decorated with mirrors may create an unwanted dressing-room effect, but large 30- by 54-inch or more panels set in a frame near a doorway, a window, or fireplace or placed in 10-inch, horizontal strips as molding, can suggest an illusion of something beyond. They can work well as a soffit detail in a high-ceilinged bathroom or as an inexpensive easy-to-clean kitchen backsplash. Mirrors also contribute interesting design solutions at a seam, where materials come together.

CONSIDER THE DISPLAY

Before making your final decision about decorating walls, consider what will be displayed on those walls—art, photographs, plaques and awards, shelving for books, or small collectibles.

White wainscoting and creams or light pastel colors are obvious choices for walls that will hold hanging collections. Small, quiet patterns work nicely with three-dimensional objects, particularly vintage curios and antiques.

Finally, remember our friends with the red dining room. Be inventive; be bold—in just one room. Bold everywhere is too much; singularly inventive is just right, just enough to catch the eye, break up the monotony, and introduce an element of surprise.

Or fun. One ultra-spirited couple redid their dining room around a magnificent Art Deco table they'd found in a SoHo shop. Instead of pasting wallpaper above the dining room chair rail, they hung pages of the Sunday funnies. The immediate perception was of a red paisley print, but upon closer inspection. . . .

When windows are small, add "presence" and light with an extra large mirror—here glued directly to the wall and surrounded by stock picture frame mouldings.

Credits: interior designer Linda Blair, ASID; photographer Peter Song

Ceilings—You Can Feel the Presence

CEILINGS USUALLY GET short shrift, unless you happen to be standing inside the Sistine Chapel. Otherwise, why bother to look up? Why indeed! In fact, even if you don't actually look up and *see* a ceiling, a ceiling plays a critical role in shaping the overall *feeling* of your room.

You can cover ceilings with the same materials as those for the walls: paint, paper, fabric, wood, tile, mirror, or lattice (very nice in a sunroom or garden room). Just be sure to use a light touch. Heavy ceilings that defy gravity press down on people's heads. Ceilings should project weightlessness.

Ceilings are not without their peculiarities. Those that are too high dehumanize; those too low, entomb. Good design compensates for a ceiling's shortcomings.

White or soft pastels slightly lighter in hue than the walls are good choices for ceilings. I'm particularly fond of pale blue, a color that follows nature. Soft colors reflect light, bathing the room with a sort of glow. Conventional ceilings—8 or 9 feet high and flat—do well with this treatment.

Ultra-high ceilings—vaulted, multiple-story, and cathedral—while truly dramatic, need careful handling to keep people from feeling dwarfed and overpowered. Darker ceiling colors often solve this spatial problem but, on the other hand, they absorb light, creating empty, hollow spaces above.

MAKE A CONNECTION

My favorite solution for too-high ceilings is to bring the ceiling color or paper down the wall from 6 to 12 inches, finishing the look with a horizontal element—a three-inch-wide painted molding, border print, stencil pattern, or mirror. The connection creates a cozy canopy effect, which works well in bedrooms, small bathrooms with high ceilings, adjoining dressing rooms, dining rooms, family rooms—any room, really.

Because we treat walls less formally today than in the past, modern walls often require little more than white paint and large expanses of windows. Nevertheless, I think souls cry out for the charm of the past, such as the intricacies of handwork seen in beautiful moldings.

Large rooms can accommodate structural elements like beams, domes, vaulted ceilings, and faux finishes, particularly *trompe l'oeil* scenes, a favorite of mine. Faux finishes add character to walls as well as ceilings, and once the finish is applied and sealed, the walls never need paint again. Like velvet, they age and mellow and look even better years later.

Faux flowers and garden scenes, with their climbing vines, adapt well to walls and ceilings. In my design studio, *trompe l'oeil* painters recreated the Tudor-style brick work visible from a window that overlooks the downtown center.

PROPORTION IS THE KEY TO WALL/CEILING MANAGEMENT

Proportion is the key to successful management of walls and ceilings. Good design can make big spaces feel more comfortable and small ones more expansive.

A few years ago, in designing my first showhouse, I inherited an unfinished, uninhabitable, and cavernous 1,200-square-foot attic storage space with a powerful presence and bizarre proportions. Crazy angles and odd alcoves protruded everywhere. A basketball court seemed the only solution.

The owner had another idea: an exercise and relaxation center with the distinctive feeling of a country home. What a challenge!

To overcome the unusual proportions (50 by 25 by 14, with a steep sloped ceiling and foreshortened walls), my staff and I established a sight line where the walls met the ceiling slope, attached a wood railing around the perimeter, and installed wainscoting below to anchor it to the floor. Then, in the 6-foot, 8-inch space between the wainscoting and ceiling line, we applied patterned fabric to stretch the space. Diminishing an awkward ceiling slope and visually lifting short walls created better scale throughout.

In the end, the room held exercise equipment, a custom bar, a media center, security equipment, and splendid furniture. We defined activity areas with inset carpet borders, furniture groupings, a rich warm color palette, well-targeted ambient and task lighting, and careful space planning. We named it The Great Escape.

While training, experience, and expertise contributed to the success of that project, simpler solutions apply to simpler situations.

The relationship of ceiling and walls is subtly enhanced through the descending ceiling fan and the ascending metal sculpture.

Credits: interior designer Joseph Braswell, ASID; photographer Ernst Beadle, dec.

B*lairstyle Tips* *for Managing Walls and Ceilings*

❖ Expand rooms with small, light, overall prints; draw rooms in with large patterns in deep colors.

❖ Make a small room appear larger with cool, pastel tints, such as shades of green, blue, and aqua.

❖ Bring walls in to cozy up an imposing space with warm, bold colors, such as yellow, red-violet, reds, and pinks.

❖ Flat matte finishes enlarge and soften space; a high gloss accents and compresses.

❖ Always use semigloss on woodwork for good adherence and easy maintenance.

❖ Pop woodwork with a slightly lighter hue, for example, eggshell with ecru, or canary with creamy yellow. I particularly like creamy whites—a delicious buttery vanilla—paired with white trim. You'll get a lovely country feeling this way while adding visual interest and a hint of tension in a quiet room.

❖ Never underestimate the power of white. And never, never say, "Just paint it white." The white palette explodes with variety in a color spectrum from warm to cool. You need only place several "whites" together to see the many gradations in tone. Every shade of white makes its own statement. Think about what you want to say.

❖ Many wallpapers come prepasted, but not sufficiently for my taste. For lasting results—and best value—instruct paperhangers to ignore the prepaste feature (if your choice comes that way) and apply the paper with paste.

❖ When hanging wood paneling, particularly on an outside wall, hang plastic sheeting first for extra insulation. You won't see it, but you'll feel the effect on cold days.

❖ Oversize rooms with high ceilings can be made more comfortable by hanging large art low on the walls. Placement creates a low focal point that balances well with the room's strong architectural presence.

❖ Lower high ceilings with horizontal elements: chair rails, wall-to-wall carpeting, or borders located below the ceiling line.

❖ A dark ceiling will not make a room look smaller. When the ceiling comes down visually, the walls appear to be pushed out, thereby increasing the perceived size.

❖ Low ceilings can be "raised" by punctuating space with vertical elements: climbing wallpaper patterns, columns, tall furniture like a highback chair, secretary, armoire, chest of drawers, headboard, or, my favorite, a screen. Available in a huge variety of designs, styles, colors and materials, screens, achieve a number of goals: A screen delineates a room within a room, making a functioning wall within walls; at the same time, it cozies up one furniture grouping while hiding another behind it. Screens are decorative as well as functional.

3
FLOORS

Consider the floor the fifth wall— the largest and most visible continuous surface in any home or office. The floor covering you choose—and where you choose to put it—is critical to lasting beauty.

—JACK FIELDS, FASID
PRESIDENT, EDWARD FIELDS, INC.

Never Underestimate What's Underfoot

WE DEMAND A lot from floors. Sticky-fingered babies, rambunctious children, active teens, acquisitive adults, and fur-shedding pets heap them with abuse. Without a moment's hesitation, we track in dirt, mud, snow, leaves, and sand, and deposit same on our floors. We jump on floors, run over them, drag things across them, drop things on them, and litter them with all manner of household collectibles, including items spiked, cleated, treaded, pointed, and grass-stained—many of them wet and dripping.

Nevertheless, we demand that floors hold up under the pressure, looking perfect 24 hours a day, 7 days a week, for years and years, without a lot of fuss, maintenance or ado on our part. These days, anything more than a quick sweep, a swish with a damp mop, or once-over-lightly with the vacuum cleaner is asking too much, even from hired help.

Now for the surprise! Floors measure up to the challenge, performing this functional magic without trickery or hocus-pocus. With thought given to life-style and such practical considerations as high traffic, food preparation and service, and access to the outdoors, for instance, floors matched to purpose will not only respond to everyday needs but will reward homeowners with versatile and glorious room design finishes and flourishes that solidify and enhance decor.

HARD FACTS ON HARD VERSUS SOFT FLOORS

Floor coverings come two ways: hard and soft, with many permutations and combinations thereof. The key to making intelligent choices is suiting the floor to the purpose. But with so many options, decision making as well as floor covering can be hard.

Floor coverings can represent a major investment. As a result, suiting the floor to the situation—one that won't knuckle under to tough treatment—represents good value for dollars spent. Hard facts will put you in a better position to make the hard decisions. Here, then, my floor-covering primer.

NATURAL STONE FOR POWER AND DRAMA

Among the hard floors, we can choose from natural stone, such as marble, granite, slate, or ceramic tile. Soft or so-called resilient floor coverings include vinyls and linoleums, natural wood, carpeting, and area rugs. Each type presents distinctive advantages, beauty features, peculiarities, and drawbacks that make it appropriate in specific situations.

Cost of materials as well as installation vary widely. Granite and marble floors are considerably more costly than ceramic tile. Natural stone substances like granite and marble, however, provide beauty and texture that vinyl can only imitate, and they will last forever.

On the other hand, granite and marble are more difficult to maintain than ceramic tile, but all three can be slippery when wet—a definite drawback in some applications. Overall, vinyl is the easiest to care for and, while it won't last forever, will prove satisfactory for quite a long time.

As we examine each type, you will begin to see how to capitalize on the strengths of each and how to use those strengths to best advantage.

❖ **Granite.** Hard floors made of natural stone such as granite, marble, and slate are expensive to purchase and install, yet deliver durability and natural elegance in kitchens, bathrooms, and entryways. Granite and marble cost two to three times more than slate, but offer more subtle patterns and long life. You'll never tire of the look.

The introduction of ¼-inch-thick tile shapes in place of stone slabs, combined with a so-called thin-set installation that eliminates the need for wire lath and a messy fixative, has made natural stone products easier and cheaper to install.

One caveat: Polished granite, like marble and high-gloss ceramic tile, is slippery when wet. Put down a mat, or specify flamed or textured granite in applications where the floor is apt to get splashed with water.

❖ **Marble.** It works in the Parthenon and it will work for you. A broad range of colors and patterned veining account for the excitement, romance, and appeal of marble. Its beauty and strength make it a wonderful choice in foyers and living rooms, but less successful in kitchens and bathrooms because it will stain unless it's sealed and waxed.

However, I often use less porous marbles (green or white) in kitchens and baths, without sealer, with good results.

Marble imported from Greece, available in small tiles from 1 to 8 inches in diameter, offers welcome variety in design. A range of soft color gradations with subtle nuances distinguishes Greek marble from that of other producing countries, and I find myself drawn to it.

❖ **Slate.** Slate is more affordable than other stone floors, but also provides durability, slip resistance, and timeless beauty. At home on outdoor patios and around pools, as well as in sunrooms, garden rooms, dens, and foyers, slate supplies beautiful colorations, picking up reds, blues, and grays from furnishings and decor. It also works wonderfully well in combination with hardwood floors.

❖ **Ceramic tile.** More costly than vinyl yet less expensive than natural stone, ceramic tile offers a rich look and a variety of designs, from ageless classics to contemporary abstracts. Tile is decorative as well as durable.

People love its color, the geometry of its shape and size, and its surface texture. By combining these features, you can create exciting tile detail in your home.

Ceramic tile is produced from a mixture of clays, which are then shaped into squares or cut into hexagonal shapes. These polygons, fired at high temperatures to bake in the color, can then be glazed and decorated, or left untreated.

Glazes, considered art forms in themselves, afford an infinite variety of colors and motifs, in finishes from matte to high gloss. Be aware, however, that glazes and sealers affect natural colors and tend to darken them.

Smooth-textured tiles in precise patterns are best suited to more formal areas. Unglazed tiles in natural clay colors, or those that mimic granite, slate, marble, and other natural stone, possess an aesthetic appeal of their own. In my view, people typically overprotect tile floors, constantly sealing and waxing for a uniform look that, in the process, destroys the charm of a natural terra cotta floor.

To use ceramic tile creatively, choose patterns and styles that relate to room theme: ceramic tiles framed in wood strips for a parquet-like effect; high-gloss tiles that underscore and define a geometrically patterned area rug; a combination of matte and polished tiles in a striped or checkerboard pattern.

Not too bold or too much, please. When it comes to decoration, simple steps provide good mileage. Insets and borders often waste tiles. Consult an installer experienced in getting the most from decorative cuts or a designer to provide the most impact in the simplest fashion.

Finally, remember that ceramic tile is a hard surface—less forgiving if you drop something and harder on your back and feet after long periods of standing. Nevertheless, if you can absorb the cost and the foundation of the room can accept the weight, choose a natural floor over a synthetic one. You'll appreciate the quality difference.

An underlayment or subfloor is required to support the added weight and provide a smooth foundation. Considerations include adequate depth to accommodate the "additional" floor, and, in a kitchen, for instance, the presence of already-installed appliances that will appear to sink to the level of the underlayment rather than stand on the new floor.

All well-planned rooms, large or small, need multiple activity areas, and this one is no exception.
Credits: interior designer Joseph Braswell, ASID; photographer Norman McGrath

Pale walls, with textured wallpaper behind the staircase, soften hard-edged architectural design.
Credits: interior designer Gail Shields-Miller; photographer Bill Rothschild

A rusticated faux finish adds special punch to a cozy corner of assorted objects; the painted floor adds elements of surprise and contrast. Both walls and floor will age surprisingly well.
Credits: interior designer Stephanie Stephens Gans; photographer Bill Rothschild

Even before Napoleon, tented rooms were
around. Here pale stripes on the walls and
ceilings add charm.

Credits: interior designer Sandra Morgan;
photographer Tim Lee

In the historic home of John Philip Sousa,
windows, doors, and the original panoramic
antique mural installed above a chair rail
interrupt the monotony of large walls.

Credits: interior designer Ann Gozo;
photographer Bill Rothschild

Stucco walls and ceiling, accentuated by strong beams and a matching stain on all the trim and woodwork, create a clean, rustic mood.
Credits: interior designer Martin Kuckly; photographer Bill Rothschild

A monochromatic scheme, produced by cream walls and ceiling, light floors, and draperies, lets our view find its way to the sea.
Credits: interior designer Martin Kuckly; photographer Bill Rothschild

(Before)
Unfortunate scale and proportions and the client's attempts at faux painting the walls in elephant gray with pink and blue, make a poor combination.

(After)
A faux finish in pale creams combines with strategically placed art designed by Westchester artist Gail Resen and Blair custom furniture to make a long narrow space with a tall ceiling feel intimate and homelike.
Credits: interior designer Linda Blair; photographer John T. Hill

Often nothing excels the character of a wood floor. The border in the style of Jean-Jacques Ruhlman, with a center medallion of Diana the huntress poised directly below the skylight, anchors the whole kitchen with the art on the floor.
Credits: interior designer John Landy, ASID; photographer Bill Rothschild

An antique Persian Sultanabad rug, with its timeless geometrics and soft colors, adds dignity and character to this gracious living room.
Credits: interior designer Linda Blair; photographer Simon Cherry

On wood or stone, a beautiful area rug helps create a welcoming mood.
Credits: interior designer Jeanne Leonard; photographer Bill Rothschild

Wood and stone alone create a magnificent pattern—here black granite and rosewood are dramatically diagonal.
Credits: interior designer Charles J. Grebmeier, ASID; photographer Russell Abraham

An unusual technique of backlighting bookcases highlights precious artifacts and burnished-leather books, poised behind a well-proportioned antique crystal chandelier.
Credits: interior designer Charles J. Grebmeier, ASID; photographer Eric A. Zepeda

Hidden light-sources create a special mood. Five well-placed lights provide magical allure—picture light to the left, candlestick lamps to the right, recessed light shining down on the table and candles glowing above it, and a glowing corner upright.
Credits: interior designer Rena Fortgang, Allied Member ASID; photographer Bill Rothschild

Custom ceiling channels create dramatic glowing light throughout this large room, balanced by hanging globes, recessed lights, and an eye-catching chandelier.

Credits: interior designer Charles J. Grebmeier, ASID; photographer Eric A. Zepeda

Contained within one of the ceiling channels, a well-crafted wooden screen filters light while it divides activities. At night, the mood changes. It's hard to tell which view is most impressive.

Credits: interior designer Charles J. Grebmeier, ASID; photographer Eric A. Zepeda

RESILIENT FLOORS FOR BEAUTY AND EASE

❖ *Vinyl tile.* Among resilient floors, vinyl is the least costly and probably the most popular choice for durability, water and stain resistance, ease of care, and design options.

Available in styles that are embossed, carved, textured, and grained, resilient vinyl flooring, a synthetic product made from vinyl resins, is an ideal choice to hide a floor's flaws and irregularities. Moreover, high-tech methods of production can create vinyl tiles that resemble marble or granite with photographic fidelity, offering an inexpensive way to dramatize entryways, hallways, and baths.

Vinyl comes in single sheets or individual squares, which can be replaced if damaged. Most sheet vinyl is easy to clean and has a built-in gloss that requires no waxing.

Vinyl patterns come inlaid or printed. Inlaid vinyl, where the pattern is applied in a series of layers and continues through the material, is much longer-lasting than printed vinyl, where patterns sit on the surface and can wear off in time.

❖ *Linoleum.* Linoleum is a natural product made from ground cork and wood, gums, pigments, and linseed oil. It comes only in printed sheets. Linoleum can't compare to vinyl in color richness or durability and is less frequently used today.

❖ *Hardwood.* Classified as resilient, hardwood floors are surprisingly inexpensive as well as safer, quieter, and easier on the legs and feet than stone or tile. Moreover, they project warmth in a classic setting, rough-hewn authenticity in rustic applications, and stability in modern decor. Their tendency to dent and scratch only adds to the patina.

Today, though, with applications of protective coatings like polyurethane, wood floors can withstand even hard use, making them effective in high-traffic areas such as entryways and family rooms, as well as a viable option in kitchens and bathrooms, where water will bead up and wipe away, leaving no telltale marks. Coating a hardwood floor makes it as easy to care for as ceramic tile, at a comparable cost.

New regulations against strong polyurethanes protect our environment, but they compromise the effectiveness of the finish. Perfection notwithstanding, the trade-off is worth it.

Most wood floors are oak, which is an attractive wood with pleasing grain patterns. Oak receives stain well and is extremely durable. Other choices in wood floors include pine, maple, walnut, and exotic woods like teak and mahogany.

Wood floor styles generally fall into two groupings: linear and parquet. Linear refers to strip flooring—narrow boards (up to about 2 inches wide) or plank flooring (from 3 to 12 inches wide), considered more rustic looking.

Parquet consists of various wood patterns created from different woods inset and glued onto a base. Despite the number of possibilities— slate, herringbone, inlaid, and basket-weave are typical looks—I never like the results. Parquet requires a proper subfloor, which adds to the cost and still doesn't always eliminate unevenness or the tendency of parquet to squeak.

Other popular hardwood options are bleached or pickled floors in which the wood grain is lightened but still visible, and plank floors inset

If subtlety is not your game, try painting a game on the floor for fun, wit, and humor in an otherwise ordinary ante-room

Credits: interior designer Diane Alpern Kovacs, Allied Member ASID; photographer Bill Rothschild

with pegs, which are reminiscent of the days when floor boards were fastened with wooden nails.

Hardwood floors can be stenciled or painted in geometric patterns or designs. *Trompe l'oeil* area rugs can be created without slippage, upkeep, dust, or allergic reactions. These painted-on-hardwood rugs offer custom decorating treatments that can be maintained with a simple dust mop. For drama, some designers are interjecting metal, vinyl, or tile into the normal pattern of the hardwood floor.

One of hardwood's biggest appeals is its longevity. Cared for properly, hardwood floors can endure for decades.

In the kitchen and dining area, the contrast of dark and light stencilling on a simple oak floor offsets stark white cabinetry.

Credits: interior designer Robert Santoro; photographer Tim Lee

Be an Informed Rug Buyer

AREA RUGS AND CARPETING

A rich variety of color, pattern, texture, and mood makes rugs and carpeting the overwhelming favorites among flooring options. Carpeting provides warmth, masks sound, and offers textures from coarse to smooth. Carpeting can become the focus of a room, or a single design element.

When buying carpeting, you must consider these elements:

- **Pile:** the length of the fibers.
- **Density:** how closely fibers are woven to each other.
- **Tufting:** how yarn is attached to the backing.
- **Twists:** how tightly fibers relate to each other.
- **Backing:** the material to which fibers are attached.
- **Weight:** overall heaviness, which helps carpets to lie flat and wear well.
- **Stain protection:** a value-added feature, important for everyday maintenance and wearability.
- **Pad:** an undercarpet to extend life; jute pads wear well, but don't provide the comfort and support of those made from urethane and foam.

Generally, carpeting refers to larger, room-size fiber floor coverings, particularly wall-to-wall; rugs are smaller and unattached, and are easily moved from one location to another. Rugs and carpeting can be either machine-tufted or hand-woven. Machine tufting is more affordable and quite durable, although you can expect to replace machine-made carpets in 10 or 12 years, or more often in high traffic areas.

HANDWOVEN RUGS FOR DESIGN AND VALUE

Quality handwoven rugs, like Orientals, can represent a sizable investment and should be purchased from reputable dealers. Unlike a computer or expensive automobile that depreciates in value from the moment of purchase, an Oriental rug will last several lifetimes. Your children will inherit your Orientals and pass them on to their children.

Because of their beauty and inherent value, Oriental rugs can be an important design element, often serving as the focal point around which your room is built.

Purchasing a handmade Oriental rug is a studied consideration. If it's within your budget, it is well worth the time and money invested. Even carpets threadbare in places represent good value and are easily resold.

Although some of the techniques involved in weaving an Oriental rug may vary from country to country, the principles of rug making are virtually the same throughout the world and, in fact, have changed very little over the centuries.

Most Oriental rugs feature a wool pile, mainly derived from sheep. After shearing, the wool is washed, carded, and then spun into yarn. Next, the yarn is dyed in an attractive range of colors and dried slowly in the sun.

A cartoon or detailed scale drawing of the carpet guides weavers throughout the making of the rug. First the rug is secured to the loom. Then the weaving begins, using either the Turkish, or symmetrical knot, or the Persian, or asymmetrical knot. With the average weaver able to tie 10,000 to 14,000 knots a day, several weavers working together need a day to complete only about an inch or so of carpet. A new carpet can take a full year to make.

At completion, the rug maker binds the edges, adds fringes, cuts the rug from the loom, and shears the carpet to create a uniform pile height. On certain carpets, particularly those from China, India, and Turkey, motifs are accented by carving or incising.

In many instances, the city or village of origin of fine Oriental rugs can be identified. Typically, village rugs consist of geometric patterns in coarser weaves that work well with more relaxed furnishings:

- **Hariz:** In northwest Iran, distinguished by a large, center me-dallion in a bold geometric design.
- **Bijar:** Smaller scale, unusual patterns, with an individual look.
- **Sultanabad:** In north central Iran; identifiable by floral designs.

Most city-woven rugs employ a close-weave technique, a center medallion, and a more complicated patterns and corners, which result in a more formal look:

- **Sarouk:** Elaborate, small-scale florals, often with center medallion.
- **Agra:** An original Indian design, not a Persian copy. Highly decorative, distinguished by use of light colors.
- **Isfahon:** In south central Iran, producer of some of the dinest Oriental rugs of woven silk and wool. Much detail.

Surely, Orientals are considered the highpoint of achievement in the genre of handwoven rugs. Other desirable examples of handweaving include Native American rugs, kilims (Turkish prayer rugs), cotton dhurries from India, painted sisals, hooked and braided rugs, needlepoint rugs, and cotton rag rugs in traditional multicolor stripes.

QUALITY VARIES IN MACHINE-TUFTING

In contrast to handweaving, where yarn is interlocked into a solid fabric, machine tufting means that yarn is punched through a preformed latex backing material light enough for tufting needles to pass through. At completion, a second backing of jute or polypropylene is laminated to the first for added stability. Quality workmanship in this process also translates to long life and good service.

Among the fibers used in rug making, wool, long-lasting, warm, resilient, and luxurious, is by far the best natural product for area rugs as well as wall-to-wall carpeting. Nylon is less expensive and also quite durable, but it lacks the depth, richness, and feel of wool. Acrylic fibers hold up, but tend to project an unnatural sheen that detracts from the overall design. Highly durable, easy-to-clean indoor–outdoor carpets, particularly useful in rec rooms, playrooms, and on porches, are more functional than attractive, but clearly serve well in given situations.

PILE DETERMINES USE

Variations in carpet pile create different design effects, suitable for different floor tasks:

- **Axminster:** a cut pile using many different colors; produces an all-purpose, long-wearing, durable carpet.

A large room pulled together by wall-to-wall broadloom with a plaid pattern reminds us that carpeting is always a good option.

Credits: interior designer Joan Spiro, ASID; photographer Bill Rothschild

- **Berber:** a nubby multilevel loop, originally handwoven by North African tribes; its rough-finished homespun style is appropriate in contemporary settings; wears extremely well.
- **Cut and loop:** mixes cut and uncut loops to achieve textures and patterns; appropriate in formal living and dining settings and in bedrooms.
- **Frisé:** tightly twisted yarns that produce a snarled configuration and nubby texture; exhibits no footmarks, shading, or shedding; when cut low and densely packed, it wears extremely well in high-traffic areas.

- **Level loop:** uncut loops of uniform height, high or low; produces an all-purpose carpet that wears well.
- **Multilevel loop:** uncut loops of varying height, producing a carved or sculpted look; best used in formal rooms.
- **Plush or velvet:** the most dense and luxurious of the cut piles, attractive in formal settings with light traffic.
- **Saxony:** a soft, dense cut pile; an all-purpose residential-use product.
- **Shag:** long pile and loose construction; it tends to mat and is hard to clean; a dated idea from the 1950s, used even then only as an accent piece more decorative than functional.

PROS AND CONS OF WALL-TO-WALL CARPETING

In the boom years following World War II, thick wall-to-wall carpeting represented the American Dream in decorating. I never shared that dream, preferring hardwood or stone floors in conjunction with dense, low-pile rugs that don't show those unsightly vacuum cleaner trails and pile reversal shadings.

Also, thick pile requires too much maintenance and attention for my taste. Because it tends to flatten, you need to rotate furnishings, getting down on your hands and knees with a brush and a hair dryer to get those matted strands to stand up. Moreover, food, dust, and small particles can get lost in a thick pile, further compromising your investment.

On the other hand, wall-to-wall carpeting provides a number of visual and practical advantages. A large expanse of carpeting stretches space while it pulls a room together. Often, however, the effect is monotonous. Wall-to-wall carpeting can be dressed up with inset borders that follow the contours of furniture and help direct traffic.

AREA RUGS DEFINE, ADD IMPACT

Area rugs define space and add impact. Colorful, patterned area rugs come in room or accent sizes. Use one under a dining room table, over a rich hardwood floor. Don't be concerned if the chairs extend beyond the rug. What matters is the proportion of floor showing and how it balances with the table.

Area rugs can also frame activity or conversation areas within a large room. Lay them right on top of wall-to-wall carpeting or a stone or hardwood floor to tie together a furniture grouping. Even a solid-colored rug with an interesting weave will unify space.

To me, the ultimate area rug is a beautiful stairway runner—a functional addition with great design power that invites you up a mosaic path.

Best use of design: Get the floor working, in the entryway, through the rooms, and up the stairs.

*B*lairstyle Tips for Choosing Floor Coverings

❖ A darker floor will help make a large room more intimate and will help light furnishings stand out more effectively.

❖ A lighter floor will help furnishings blend into the overall scheme. You can lighten up dimly lit rooms with pale shades that reflect color. Conversely, use light-absorbing deeper tones in well-lit interiors.

❖ A small dark place, like a hallway or alcove, can be dramatized with an intense color. Colors that would be overwhelming in rooms where you spend a lot of time can be energizing in small doses. Be bright and showy in dining rooms and foyers but never in bedrooms.

❖ Color affects mood. Warm colors create an atmosphere of friendliness and cheer, whereas cool colors are more refreshing and clean. The best combinations incorporate warm and cool colors; however, it's best to allow one color temperature to dominate.

❖ Texture affects the look of any color. Smooth surfaces will appear lighter and rough ones darker. Brighten up a dimly lit room with a polished surface; tone down the glare of a sunny room with a matte finish.

❖ When planning the layout of a tiled floor, remember that vertical lines add energy to a room and lengthen it. Diagonals create a feeling of dynamism and motion, which also adds depth. Curved or circular patterns add openness and flow to restricted spaces.

❖ In high-use areas—entries, halls, stairs, kitchens, baths, family rooms—choose resilient floor coverings or heavy-duty carpeting. In low-use areas—bedrooms, formal living rooms, dining rooms—use delicate colors and plush surfaces with patterned accents.

❖ Wall-to-wall carpeting unifies and enlarges space; area rugs define space.

❖ Always view products in place; select rugs and carpeting from samples "on the floor," not on a table or platform. (By the same token, don't hold wallcovering flat against carpeting; place it vertically.)

❖ For best results, flooring materials should blend from room to room and along connecting pathways, as well as within each room. Avoid jarring contrasts underfoot, unless it's a jewel of an occasional area rug.

❖ In general, follow nature's path: darker floors and medium walls with ceilings that are lighter, like the sky.

4
LIGHTING

Spirit and soul should define a space, not a room label. Interior design can create intimacy where seemingly there was none; it can change darkness to light; it can dramatize or understate. As such, design is illusion. Lighting design, in particular, can change what we see and how we see it.

—CHARLES J. GREBMEIER, ASID
SAN FRANCISCO

Lighting Becomes an Exciting Design Element with a Thoughtful Blending of Creative and Electrical Juices

LIGHTING, THE MOST ELUSIVE of all design elements, works subliminally, playing on the subconscious rather than the conscious mind. Instinctively, we move toward light. As surely as sunshine on a beautiful day draws us outdoors, a well-lighted room beckons and welcomes us as we enter.

Like art, lighting communicates—conveying its message through a series of techniques that are hard to observe. The power of a painting to transfix, of music to transport, of literature to transcend hinges on the talent of the painter or musician or writer, not on your personal expertise in color, composition or narrative drive.

Similarly, the power of lighting to affect quality of life is unrelated to your perception of light source, strength of wattage or balance of illumination. Yet the application of these techniques in proper proportion can induce a feel-good quality that makes you smile—and wonder why.

On a purely functional level, lighting illuminates. It makes dark areas brighter so that people can see what they're doing and go where they're going without falling and hurting themselves. Certainly safety is an important aspect of responsible room design, but to stop there is to deny yourself and the interior spaces you inhabit the positive benefits of the aesthetic properties of artificial light.

In my experience, most people choose lighting fixtures for their decorative quality alone. Lamps become furniture, their light-delivering capabilities something of an afterthought. An unusually shaped floor lamp may provide drama, but will it provide enough light for reading? A beautiful chandelier with cut-glass teardrops may add a starlit effect to dinner parties, but will it shroud the sideboard and china cabinet in shadow?

In fact, the lighting industry has developed a number of functional improvements in recent years that team aesthetics and practicality so that the buying public can purchase decorative lamps that illuminate well and manage shadow and glare, while keeping utility and bulb replacement costs down. The result: good design and good value for the consumer.

WELL-LIT ROOMS BLEND THREE TYPES OF LIGHTING

A brief lesson on types and sources of lighting and an overview of fixtures and practical applications will facilitate intelligent buying. First, let's straighten out some terminology, and then we'll look at the three basic types of lighting: ambient, accent, and task.

What the average consumer refers to as bulbs and fixtures lighting professionals call lamps and luminières. It's important to recognize the distinction when you begin shopping for lighting equipment. You may find it confusing to go into a lighting store and ask to see lamps, only to be shown bulbs. Because it's comfortable and familiar, we can continue our discussion of lighting using the customary bulb-fixture terminology.

Now, types of light:

❖ *Ambient.* Ambient light is overall light that spreads soft, general illumination in a room, and provides a relaxing atmosphere. Ambient lighting produces interesting effects by bathing walls, ceilings, or draperies with light, by downlighting from a series of well-spaced, recessed ceiling spots, by using perimeter or cove lighting around a room, or by using large-area light sources or chandeliers in the center ceiling.

Rooms "feel" nice with good ambient light. Ambient light encourages dialogue in living rooms without creating an overbright onstage sensation, promotes intimate discussion in dining rooms, and helps shut the daily madness out of bedrooms.

Ambient light from a standing lamp with halogen light can enlarge space by giving ceilings a push upward, or humanize overly high ceilings with dropped ceiling fixtures that only hint at the space above.

❖ *Accent.* Accent or directional lighting focuses attention. It dramatizes specific areas and separates one from another. You can create accent lighting with track-mounted, recessed or surface mounted lighting fixtures, used in combination with ambient light.

You don't want your living room to look like a gymnasium, with bright light from one end to the other. Accent lights can focus on simple objects or collections, pieces of furniture, or greenery arrangements, pointing up their beauty. At the same time, accent lights provide peripheral illumination that becomes an easy segue for the eye as it looks away from these high points. The combination of soft ambient light overall and hot spots for drama provides a sense of rhythm and movement in large spaces.

❖ *Task.* Task lighting does just that—gives you a better look at the task you're performing. Reading, writing, sewing, and cooking are task-oriented activities that require a balance of strong, diffused light without glare, close to the task at hand. I've won over many clients ny promising to provide a comfortable chair and good reading light—something they've never had.

As we get older, we require more light to see properly, especially for tasks. A comfortable reading light level for teenagers probably seems shadowy to their parents.

Task light is best when it's directed over the shoulder. For instance, for a bedroom redesign I selected high chests instead of low night tables to flank the bed, thereby creating an over-the-shoulder platform for reading in bed. The clients love the look, which is very different from nightstands or an over-the-headboard wall-attached light, and they appreciate the ease on the eyes.

A WORD ABOUT ENERGY CONSERVATION

All rooms need ambient light, most require task lighting, and many benefit from accent lighting. Using all three—of the same coloration—in a single room creates a pleasant atmosphere that responds to utilitarian needs as well as design interest. And with today's energy-saving bulbs, no room need be underlit in the interest of saving money or conserving energy.

I can still picture my father going around the house turning off lights. "You think we're majority stockholders in the electric company?" he'd ask.

People still complain about the high cost of electricity, but in fact lighting accounts for only a fraction of your monthly utility bill. Heat-generating appliances—clothes dryers, hair dryers, toasters—are the real culprits.

Certainly, you should turn off lights you're not using, but be sure to have enough light programmed into your rooms so that it's there when you need it.

COMBINE TYPES OF LIGHT
WITH SOURCES OF LIGHT

Now let's examine light sources. Then we'll look at fixtures and finally put all the information together into individual room settings.

❖ *Incandescent.* Incandescent light, such as that from an ordinary table lamp, produces a warm glow that most closely approximates daylight. While attractive and appealing, incandescents have a relatively short life, only about 100 hours.

Always somewhere in the house, it seems, a burned-out bulb needs replacing. True, replacing a bulb in a table lamp is a quick and easy job, but it's a nuisance when you're busy or entertaining guests.

Blown ceiling bulbs turn into an operation—dragging out a ladder, removing the globe, changing the bulb, replacing the globe, up the ladder, down the ladder, and finally putting the ladder away. This process moves beyond nuisance to irritation.

I know a couple who replace every ceiling bulb twice a year—in April and October, on the Sundays they adjust their clocks to initiate and cancel Daylight Saving Time—simply to avoid the chore throughout the year. For myself, I find this an onerous, and unnecessarily costly, way to spend a Sunday. Nevertheless, the thinking illustrates a drawback of incandescent light.

❖ *Fluorescent.* Fluorescent lighting produces up to five times as much light as incandescent light for the same energy expended, and it can last in excess of 10,000 hours. Although fluorescents are initially more expensive to purchase, they cost considerably less over the long haul.

Early fluorescents produced an unflattering cool light, but the introduction of small PL lamps (bulbs) has vastly improved their quality. These new PL lamps, available in a wide color spectrum of cool to warm, are particularly effective in wall sconces, where a bright, long lasting and inexpensive light works well.

Fluorescent tubes are available in warm-white tones in up to six-foot lengths. These "sticks" add bright, cheery, long-lasting light as well as visually appealing design features when covered with what I call the "Chiclet®" ceiling fixture. This molded plastic covering, which looks like a giant chewing gum Chiclet suspended from the ceiling, adapts well to many design styles, and drops like a trap door on one side for easy tube replacements. No matter, you won't need to use the trap door very often.

❖ *Halogen.* Halogen lights, which burn about 3,000 hours, combine the warmth of incandescents with the long life of fluorescents. A tiny halogen lamp, powered by a transformer, can ricochet off the ceiling with enough strength to light up a large room.

A TRIP TO THE TYPICAL LIGHTING STORE

Now that you can classify types and sources of light, it's time to look at the major categories of fixtures available in lighting stores. With this information, you will be able to make appropriate lighting decisions for the rooms in your home.

Basic knowledge about lighting will also help you work more effectively with design professionals, who are experienced in applying technical data in residential settings for optimal practical and decorative effects.

The typical lighting store is a confusing mass of fixtures—pendant after pendant, chandelier after chandelier, floor lamps, table lamps, wall sconces everywhere. Each category is designed to solve different lighting problems in different lighting situations. The embarrassment of riches doesn't help novice buyers, many of whom can't isolate one fixture from all the rest, much less project its effect into their own room setting.

Moreover, most shopowners set up display fixtures with 25-watt bulbs. Before you buy any fixture, ask to see it powered to full wattage. Would you buy a car without a test drive?

❖ *Permanent versus portable fixtures.* A major decision about fixtures is whether you will own or rent. Floor and table lamps that can be moved from room to room, or packed up and taken with you when you move from one location to another, are portable. You own them. Lights recessed into the ceiling are permanent. Essentially, you rent them for as long as you live at a location and then leave them for the next homeowner or tenant.

Track lighting, made up of cones and heads that hang from a track attached to a wall or ceiling, is what I call leased lighting, offering you the option to take it with you or turn it back at the end of your stay—like a leased car that you can purchase or return at the completion of the contract.

Similarly, wall sconces, while easier to handle than long tracks of lights, present the same take-it–or–leave-it dilemma.

That a fixture belongs to the room rather than your estate is no reason to stint on quality. While you inhabit the space, you should have the advantage of the best lighting solution and aesthetic appeal that you can comfortably afford. When you sell or relocate, your bank book will realize the rewards of your good judgment.

❖ *Recessed fixtures.* Recessed ceiling lights and cove lights implanted in walls provide even, ambient light with a positioning advantage. Heads can be pointed in specific directions for interesting as well as practical effects.

❖ *Track lighting.* Track lighting is less expensive and somewhat more adaptable than recessed lights, but track systems, which hang from the ceiling, are also more obtrusive.

Nevertheless, multiple head shapes provide design interest and can address ambient, task and accent lighting from the same installation. Also, because the heads are free, they can rotate a full 180 degrees for more flexible positioning. Many galleries employ track lighting for its illumination options and design interest.

It's important, however, that you have ample height, or the ceiling may feel top heavy.

❖ *Wall sconces.* Lighting with wall sconces is a favorite choice of mine because, like cove lighting around a room near the ceiling, sconces provide upper light. I custom-design sconces to blend with period or contemporary styles, or retrofit existing fixtures to maintain vintage charm with modern, code-compliant light sources and wiring.

❖ *Floor lamps.* The torchère is the long-reigning king of floor lamps—a slim stick with a torch-shaped shade that opens up to the ceiling, bouncing soft, reflected light back into the room. The torch lamp helps to "elevate" low ceilings.

Downlight floor lamps satisfy reading and study tasks. Modern-looking halogen versions complement contemporary settings, bathing activity areas with more light than would seem possible from such tiny sources.

❖ *Table lamps.* Table lamps are like art or sculpture. They decorate as well as illuminate. Choose lamps that harmonize with furnishings, shades proportional in size to lamp height, and shade materials that add texture without interfering with light flow. Remember, too, that the shade color looks different when the lamp is turned on.

❖ *Hanging fixtures.* Pendant lamps and chandeliers hang from the ceiling on a cord or chain, high enough to clear heads, or about 30 inches above a table. You can match styles to any decor—heavily ornate to machine modern, Italian Renaissance to French provincial, Early American to Art Deco. And, of course, wonderful Tiffany shades add an opalescent stained-glass effect.

❖ *Uplights.* A form of accent lighting, uplights, attach to walls or shine light upward from tabletop canisters. Uplight, as opposed to downlight from hanging fixtures and table lamps, provides artistic effects in connection with artwork and sculpture displays. It also works well behind plants and in some furniture groupings. Place carefully, however, to avoid shadows.

MAKING THE MOST OF LIGHT

Now it's time to take what we've learned and apply it to individual rooms. Naturally, every room is different and every lighting situation is unique. But some general guidelines will get your creative juices flowing.

❖ *Living rooms.* In the living room, use a combination of wall washers, floor lamps, small recessed ceiling lights and cove lights for general ambient illumination. Spotlights and table lamps provide good reading light, while hot spots that are at least three times brighter than ambient light can accent art, collections, an antique, or an unusual plant. Balance light so that accents appear around the room, not weighted to one side, and help the eye make easy transitions from one area to another.

Variety in lighting levels facilitates different tasks and moods. Control light from wall switches at the entrance to the living room, some on a dimmer to allow a choice of mood. Place lamps so that the shade protects the eye from the source while directing light to the task.

❖ *Dining rooms.* A chandelier or pendant light is a dining room natural. With benefit of a dimmer switch, a subtle center-of-the-ceiling light can draw in diners for intimate suppers or, with the wattage turned up, encompass larger gatherings. Remember, though, dining means food. I don't think it destroys the mood to be able to see what you're eating.

Place dimmer-controlled ceiling spots at the perimeter to balance the center fixture, eliminate shadows on people's faces, and provide the depth for wall-hugging dining room furniture pieces.

For drama, use a carefully directed, narrowly focused accent light to highlight the table centerpiece.

❖ *Kitchens.* Flood kitchens with light. Working with sharp knives and hot sauces in dim light invites accidents.

Start with good task lighting from recessed ceiling lights beamed on countertops and cooking surfaces and light that is recessed under soffits and cabinets. Then balance it with general ambient light sourced from

big fluorescent ceiling tubes and pendants. Spreading illumination evenly in all the nooks and crannies makes your kitchen brighter, happier, and safer.

❖ *Family rooms.* Today's multiactivity family room requires a carefully thought-out lighting plan that responds to television watching as well as homework and computing, game playing and snacking, and family confabs and entertaining.

Consider recessed and hanging ceiling fixtures, wall washers, and cove lights, teamed with task lighting from pendants and, perhaps, a track lighting system for direct light on hobbies, games, and office/school work. All are needed to do the job right. Be careful that light on laminated

Hidden light sources, especially overhead, create a special atmosphere the way a blue sky does on a summer day. Ambient lighting in a domed dining room ceiling, reinforced by strategically placed pairs of recessed lights, is offset by a candlelit living room and patio beyond.

Credits:
interior designer Vince Lattuca; photographer Bill Rothschild

game boards and computer screens doesn't create shadows or glare. Baffles that shield the light source will help. Place a reading lamp beside a chair or sofa.

Families spend inordinate amounts of time in family rooms—hence the name. Proper lighting will contribute to household productivity and good times.

❖ **Bedrooms.** Soft light that shelters bedrooms from the world's harsh realities makes for restful sanctuaries, but it falls short for reading and other closeup tasks, like putting on makeup or replacing a broken shoelace.

For best results, augment general ambient light with good reading light installed at bedside or over the headboard, and two vertical columns of light at the dressing table.

Other possibilities: Install soft cove lights for a hint of romance; retrofit vintage wall sconces with halogen bulbs to update the charm of period decor; hang incandescent bulb fixtures in closets—they most closely approximate natural light—to reduce the does-this-go-with-that scramble.

❖ **Bathrooms.** Even the smallest bathroom requires two levels of light for proper illumination. At the sink, a light level of 70 footcandles is the minimum for shaving or makeup application.

When light hits a protrusion in the face, such as a large forehead or cheekbones, the rest of the face falls into shadow. To counteract the effect, use continuous light across the top and down the sides of the mirror, like you'd find in an actor's dressing room.

If space won't permit lighting three sides of your mirror, mount a 48-inch horizontal light strip above the mirror, or install sconces on either side of the mirror, not less than 30 inches apart. To balance this side light, add a downlight from the ceiling, as close to the mirror as possible.

In the bathroom, avoid halogen bulbs; instead choose soft, widespread light in the 85–90 CRI (Color Rendering Index) range. (Cool white fluorescent lighting measures only a 72 CRI.) Also, choose light-colored countertops and wall colors that reflect rather than absorb light.

Lighting the sides of your face is important for proper illumination as well as self-esteem. Glare and shadow are the culprits here, and you should design a bathroom light plan to avoid them.

Use soft light (a 50-footcandle level is adequate) over a whirlpool tub; it will help you to relax. Use wall washers on side and back walls, and install a dimmer switch to help cushion the blow when you first enter in the morning.

❖ *Passages.* Entryways, foyers, and halls point the way, serving as warm preludes to the rooms beyond. Safety and practicality rather than mood lighting are the key here, but don't overlook the double-duty opportunities. Highlight art on the walls or a photographic display up the stairs with accent lights that illuminate the passageway as well as your good taste.

B*lairstyle Tips on Room Lighting*

❖ **Create balanced light. Distractions like shadow and glare can affect equilibrium, orientation, attention span and short-term memory.**

❖ **To reduce glare, use materials that are poor light reflectors. Instead of shiny walls, floors, cabinets, tables, and countertops, made from marble, chrome, and glass, seek out textured surfaces, like flamed granite and unsealed ceramic tile.**

❖ **Avoid eyestrain by turning on a light when watching television.**

❖ **Conduct routine lighting checkups. Reposition "slipped" accent spots; adjust wattage to accommodate new room colors that may absorb or reflect more light; clean fixtures, shades, reflectors and bulbs.**

❖ **Locate exterior lighting so that it doesn't shine through windows.**

❖ **If the fixture can handle it, change a reflector bulb to a PAR bulb to double the brightness output.**

❖ **Full-spectrum daylight simulating light sources have been shown to have a positive impact on well-being. The results: better visual acuity, less physiological fatigue, lower breathing and pulse rates, and mood elevation.**

*B*lairstyle Tips
on Lighting for the Elderly

❖ Older people need more light to achieve visual acuity. In lighting for the aged, be distinct rather than subtle.

❖ Light levels appropriate for a healthy 20-year-old will double for a healthy 60-year-old.

❖ Avoid high contrast levels between task and ambient lighting.

❖ Treat lighting for seniors the same as any other barrier-free design requirement: Use light to indicate upcoming changes, to direct people through spaces, such as steps, elevators, door thresholds, and ramps. Visual warnings eliminate surprises and prevent accidents.

❖ The elderly typically see a "step" between a dark bedroom and a well-lit hallway. Avoid accidents with soft transitions like bedroom nightlights and illuminated wall switches.

❖ For reading at close range, a 75-watt bulb positioned directly over the shoulder is adequate for most older people with good vision; for those with poor vision, use a 100-watt bulb.

❖ Paint interior walls lighter colors that reflect more light.

❖ Prune back plants in front of windows to let in every ray of natural light.

❖ When installing new light fixtures, choose pull-down types for easy maintenance and bulb replacement rather than fixed-position types that require a ladder.

❖ Remember, older people suffer reduction in pupil size and loss of focusing ability. To them, bright light is equal to wearing medium-density sunglasses. In dim light, older people feel they are wearing extremely dark sunglasses.

5

WINDOWS AND DOORS

Just as the human eye acts as a window to the soul, windows in general serve as conduits between daylight and its ability to dramatize and uplift interior spaces. Today's manufacturing methods build in efficiency and performance features as well as strong architectural assets, making the window one of a room's most rewarding design elements.
—LLOYD BELL, FASID
NEW YORK CITY

With So Many Options Available Today, Choosing a Window Is No Longer an Open and Shut Case

WINDOWS: WE TAKE them for granted—opened to let in fresh air, closed to keep out the chill. In fact, these are important, necessary, but secondary functions. Primarily, windows control the amount of natural light that enters a space, and natural light, perhaps more than any other design element, shapes quality of life.

Before 1908, when building codes were enacted to spell out specific conditions under which people could live comfortably, safely, and heathfully, amenities such as natural light were largely ignored. Tall tenement buildings that sprang up side by side, one blocking the other's light, produced dark and dreary interiors that exacerbated dark and dreary lives.

Now, we know better. Natural light, with all its attributes, cannot solve all of life's problems, but it gives a big boost to health and happiness. Entering through thoughtfully planned doors and windows, natural light illuminates rooms in a soft glow that can relax the body, elevate the mood, and relieve stress. We need only provide the proper openings to let in the magic.

Keep in mind, too, that unlike any other design element, a window provides exterior as well as interior detail. Whether you are thinking about updating your home or putting on a new addition, you should give considerable thought to windows for design interest as well as energy efficiency.

TAKE A WINDOW TOUR

An exercise I like to recommend is a window tour of the neighborhood. Get into your car and take a drive up and down the streets, looking specifically at how different styles of windows make building facades more interesting and appealing.

You'll find that with so many options available today, choosing a window is no longer an open and shut case.

❖ *Double-hung.* As you drive through various neighborhoods, you'll see double-hung windows on many older homes. These windows consist of two sections, one that moves up from the bottom, and the other that opens down from the top. The top window typically is fitted out with six small individual panes of glass (two rows of three), divided and held in place by wood moldings called *muntins* or *mullions*.

This charming feature, called true-divided lights, is imitated today by window manufacturers who provide window moldings in the shape of true-divided lights that snap on and off large panes of glass for easy cleaning, or that come embedded between two panes of glass. Although not as elegant, they make cleaning a breeze, particularly if the window has the open-in feature that lets you clean the outside from the inside. Yet while we like the easy-maintenance features of the modern version, frankly nothing quite compares to the real thing, which, unfortunately, is an expensive option in today's marketplace.

Curiously, true-divided lights represent a purely practical holdover from the past, before modern technology provided the formula for great expanses of glass without dividers.

❖ *Casement.* Another commonly seen window style is the *casement*. Here, the sash is hinged at the side and opens by swinging in or out. Casement windows are by nature plain, but they can be fitted with custom grilles or topped with half-round or elliptical windows or rectangular transom windows to achieve grand and elegant effects.

On your tour, you'll see that modest homes take on character with well-suited window detailing, just as large homes can appear naked with colorless windows.

Stained-glass church windows, while too imposing for comfort in residential applications, nevertheless teach valuable window lessons. Their size provides focus; interesting window tops—angles and semi-circles—supply dramatic effect, and the stained-glass art form, again overwhelming for home use, introduces a marvelous window detail—in small doses. I find that builders sometimes get carried away with too many window styles in a single structure. Discipline and taste should prevail.

❖ *Art glass.* A stained-glass panel inset in a casement window, for instance, becomes an exciting visual feature that, when coordinated with the angle of the sun, encourages kaleidoscopic lighting effects within the space. Capitalizing on the art form, manufacturers are producing a line of so-called art-glass insets with graceful stained-glass trims and edge patterns that introduce formal design without interfering with the flow of natural light.

❖ *Bay windows.* You can create cozy niches for reading or nature watching from a window seat, while adding an architectural detail, with the addition of a bay or bowed-out window. Using this technique in a small kitchen, I was able to bring natural light into cramped quarters and transform the kitchen from business-only to eat-in, all with a modest 24-inch addition.

A small window installation project provided value that the home-owners appreciate every day and that will reimburse them many times over when they decide to sell.

❖ *Transom windows.* Square- or rectangular-shaped windows that push out from the bottom make attractive window and door toppers. Old-fashioned office corridors with textured doors (found in vintage detective movies) always had transom windows that opened at the top for ventilation, a style that gave rise to the expression about business coming in unexpectedly "over the transom." Typically opened by someone standing on a stepladder or using a window pole, transom windows now come motorized, operated from a convenient wall switch.

A spinoff idea on the old-fashioned transom window is to add a row of windows *under* kitchen cabinets, in the space usually reserved for a backsplash. I also like a large window that descends all the way to the sink, with no backsplash except for a few inches.

❖ *Skylights.* Natural light from above simulates a natural environment. Skylights, usually casement or transom windows mounted in ceilings or roofs, act like the sunroof of a car that affords natural light during the day, moon glow at night, and fresh air anytime. A modern phenomenon, skylights tend to infringe on the character of older neighborhoods. Also they must be of top-notch construction or they will leak.

Skylights, for all their advantages, are unsightly when viewed from the front of the house and should be relegated to rear roofs only; also, they should be flat. Domed skylights tend to resemble tiny tombs and should be avoided.

Watch for double-hung and casement windows, unusual window toppers and custom grilles, and bay, transom, and skylight windows, among other special effects on your window tour.

THE PERSONALITY OF LIGHT

Architects and interior designers familiar with window shapes, sizes, and properties can suggest window groupings that complement various architectural styles, as well as appropriate trims—such as pediments, arches, and keystones—that give a finished look to window installations.

Designers also study space to take full advantage of the personality of natural light that filters through windows. Indeed, like you, light—at different times of the day and from different exposures—displays dispo-

A 90's window drama offers a cozy upstairs landing with a commanding view of the outside terrain

Credits:
interior designer Jeanne Leonard;
photographer Bill Rothschild

sition, temper, and mood. Careful application of the properties of light through suitable window vehicles transfers assets to your rooms.

Kitchens and breakfast nooks that catch the rising sun seem cheery, while bedrooms, dining rooms, porches, patios, and decks flourish in spectacular sunsets. Family rooms bubble over in upbeat southern light, while diffused northern light nourishes dens and hideaways. Placing windows to capture natural light and then releasing the light to cascade through residential space is, perhaps, the designer's finest hour.

New homes and renovations often feature tall windows with circle tops and transoms. Creative window treatment starts up high and bravely includes stripes.

Credits:
interior designer Linda Blair, ASID; photographer Kurt A. Dolnier

The romance of natural light and the desire to bask in its warmth have created a demand for larger windows that proclaim nature's bounty and, at the same time, blur the line between the indoors and outdoors. These lighter, airier spaces with their important window displays demand improved performance from windows. In the past, the bigger the windows, the more it cost you to maintain a comfortable temperature in your home. Happily, manufacturers have responded with some amazing innovations.

IMPROVEMENTS IN WINDOW PERFORMANCE

Older homes, where time and weather have rusted out fittings and cracked many of the installation moldings, are particularly vulnerable to weather leaks that let in winter's cold and summer's heat. These leaks also let heat and air conditioning escape with the result that, in spite of soaring energy costs, the homes are still chilly in the winter and close in the summer.

However, giant strides in window technology have opened up a world of new options for today's homeowners. Energy conservation in conjunction with style plays a more prominent role in home building and remodeling than ever before. Sophistication is the hallmark of window aesthetics as well as performance.

❖ *U-values.* To begin, those in the market for new windows should learn about U-values, a measurement of thermal efficiency based on a window's resistance to the flow of energy. Simply put, the lower the U-value, the more energy-efficient the window.

Most new window technology has been directed toward lowering U-values without adding extra panes. Windows constructed of more than two panes generally are considered cumbersome and difficult to clean.

As a result, window manufacturers are focusing their efforts on increasing the thermal performance of the dual-pane glass window unit. The most significant of these developments are heat-resistant window-edge seals, energy-saving glass coatings, and improved insulation with argon gas.

❖ *Window-edge seals.* Dual-pane windows are constructed with edge spacers that separate the two panes. Until recently, most window manufacturers used large aluminum edge spacers. However, because metal conducts energy, these spacers contributed significantly to the increase in U-values around the edge of a window.

Today, many window manufacturers are converting to a new type of edge spacer, constructed of a wafer-thin, corrugated aluminum strip embedded in a sealant. This edge spacer is made with moisture-sealing, heat-resistant polymers that reduce the flow of heat around the window edge and prevent condensation from forming between the panes.

The system is designed not only to keep the window edge warmer during cold weather but also to reduce the flow of heat into the home during the hot summer months and year round in warm climates.

❖ *Low-E coatings.* A second factor to consider when selecting windows is a relatively new development based on low-emissivity technology, referred to in the marketplace as low-E glass. This is glass that is coated with a metallic film that improves a window's thermal performance by allowing light to pass through freely while blocking the passage of heat.

Essentially, low-E technology reflects heat radiation back into the home, keeping the inside temperature of the window glass warmer. It also prevents heat from beating in on hot, sultry summer days. As a result, coated glass helps to conserve energy and reduce heating and air conditioning costs.

As a bonus, low-E coatings also reduce harmful ultraviolet rays that cause carpeting and upholstery to fade.

❖ *Argon gas.* Argon gas, the same colorless, inert gas used in ordinary incandescent light bulbs, is now also used by many window manufacturers to replace the air between insulating glass panes. Because argon gas is heavier than air, it is a better insulator.

Nevertheless, gas is thin and can escape—like helium from a balloon. Only top-quality window construction and sealants will keep argon gas from slowly seeping out from between the panes. As long as the gas remains in place, U-values will remain low.

❖ *Wood versus aluminum window frames.* Although wood window frames were the industry standard for years, a number of manufacturers now produce windows in aluminum, a light-weight, durable, weather-resistant material that serves well with little or no maintenance.

Aluminum, however, is a less efficient insulator. It draws heat from the room toward the cold surface and contributes to that chill you feel on cold, damp days.

Wood, on the other hand, holds in heat, but although an excellent insulator, performing many hundreds of times more efficiently than aluminum, it requires regular maintenance—stripping, sealing, and painting—to look its best.

❖ *Vinyl-clad wood frames.* A relatively new development, these provide the advantages of wood insulation with the maintenance-free features of aluminum. Also available are windows that are vinyl-clad outside for ease of maintenance and wood inside for better aesthetics.

NEW AND NOTEWORTHY

Other noteworthy window features recently introduced include what I call the "mini-blind sandwich" and the "foggy bottom."

❖ *The mini-blind sandwich* is just that—a mini-blind implanted between two panes of glass. The result: You get both the sweep of a bare window, and the clean, contemporary look of a mini-blind when you want privacy, plus easy maintenance. Bonus: The mini-blind slats—dust catchers par excellence—stay forever clean in their sealed sandwich state.

❖ *The foggy bottom* window provides a choice: a view or complete privacy at the flip of a switch. A thin film of liquid crystals encapsulated between two sheets of laminated glass creates the fog when the crystals make a random pattern. When you turn on the electricity, however, the crystals line up, and voila! The glass is clear. Turn the power off for frosted glass; turn it on for a view.

I've seen a foggy bottom topped with a nontreated half-round window fitted with a fan-pattern custom grille. This is an attractive and functional bit of technologic wizardry, particularly appropriate in a bathroom.

WINDOW AESTHETICS

Window aesthetics have improved right along with practicality. In fact, some new designs are dramatic enough to suggest leaving windows bare, at least during the day. For nighttime privacy, roll-up shades may be all that's needed.

Full-circles, half-rounds, quarter-rounds, trapezoids, and other geometric window shapes add design interest as well as curb appeal. Large, dramatic expanses in casement and cathedral styles complement grand entryways and multistory great rooms. By the same token, a series of small windows can humanize ungainly space. Window size can make a too-small room seem larger, create a focal point for boxy spaces, or carve a romantic niche out of an awkward alcove. With the right window and a chair, you can turn wasted space into a private hideaway.

Finish windows with custom grilles, patterns, and stained-glass effects, and even the simple double-hung window takes on new grace.

There are windows to match every architectural style—from Colonial to Tudor, from Victorian to contemporary. For best results, suit the window to the style. While mix-and-match, eclectic interiors work, architecture is best left pure.

Casement windows are typically French or English Tudor, while double-hung windows with pretty grilles grace Spanish and Colonial homes. Large, dramatic expanses of windows, with geometric toppers, complement expansive contemporaries, whereas a series of small windows provide plenty of natural light without overpowering a modest ranch or split-level.

Keep in mind that cost generally increases proportionate to size. Nevertheless, as windows represent a test of quality in your home, replacing them is an affordable way to upgrade appearance, comfort, and value.

Doors—First Impressions Count

THE FRONT DOOR sets the tone for what's inside. A mediocre door with inferior hardware that doesn't work properly reflects poorly on you and your standards. A front door creates a first impression, and first impressions—no matter what follows—are lasting.

A front door also can make a bold statement. Elizabeth Arden understands the power of the front door. Hers are signature red.

Let's say you're in the market for a new car. There you are in the showroom, surrounded by cars, all bright and shiny. You can look under the hood and kick the proverbial tires, but what have you learned? Then you open the car door, look inside, and swing the door shut. Ah, now you know something. You like the sound of the door when it closes. It feels right. It has a certain heft, a solid resonance.

So should your front door. Like a piece of silver or a favorite utensil, it must have a good feel, a good look, a proper tone.

Growing up, I remember the doormen at our building always polishing the brass. Those big doors with their gleaming fittings gave me great pleasure and a sense of pride about my home.

Front doors must be made of solid wood with good hardware. Quality counts. Think of the *feng shui* concept of the front door as a gateway to the lives of those inside. Choose the right wood stain or paint color for your door, and select appropriate plantings to create a welcoming entrance.

INTERIOR DOORS

Inside your home, solid wood doors with etched panels and good hardware project quality throughout.

Bi-fold or louvered doors provide ventilation and screening for laundry areas, activity centers, and closets.

French doors add elegance to dining room entrances and, because they're constructed of glass panes that extend for most of the length, can double as windows.

And big sliding-glass doors that open to your patio or deck bring the beauty of the outdoors indoors.

Blairstyle Tips on Selecting Windows and Doors

❖ Never assume that any window you buy today comes equipped with the latest performance, comfort, and efficiency features. Not all do. After a window is installed is no time to discover that the product you've chosen is drafty, or that it allows heat to escape or condensation to form between the panes. These problems detract from a window's aesthetic quality and also reduce its energy efficiency and overall value.

❖ Remember that a window is the single design element that makes an interior as well as an exterior statement. Consider a window purchase from both points of view.

❖ It's difficult to select windows from a catalog; you need to see them in real-life applications. Take the neighborhood tour and observe the look of the windows. Once you narrow down the style choices, you can talk with window experts about the performance of particular manufacturers' brands.

❖ When placing windows in new installations, consider outdoor view as well as interior placement.

❖ Consider the door as a gateway to your home and the lifestyle you enjoy within. A regal, solid door is a symbol of quality.

6
FABRIC AND WINDOW TREATMENTS

Fabric contributes a revealing touch about an individual—a level of sophistication, tactile disposition, color preferences as well as intensities and shades. How fabric dresses a window—often the element that establishes that all-important first impression— can set the mood of the entire room.
—BARBARA SCHLATTMAN, ASID
HOUSTON

As Hair Frames a Face, Window Treatments Should Frame the Opening, Not Hang in Front of It

EDITH WHARTON, in one of her more acerbic accounts of society, railed against the Victorians and their claustrophobically overdressed windows, declaring that no window treatment at all was probably the best one. Wharton was definitely on to something here.

Examine your room. Maybe the view is wonderful and the room situated so that neighbors can't peer in, even at night when lighting against uncovered windows makes it seem as though you're living in a fishbowl. Perhaps you live in a moderate temperature zone where bare windows won't allow cold air to seep in or heated air to leak out. If you're never inconvenienced by the sun streaming in laser-like across your primary seating area and never disturbed by outside noises intruding on your peace and serenity, then by all means leave your windows bare, particularly if they provide their own style statement.

Unfortunately, most rooms fall prey to at least one or maybe all of those perils: a poor view, lack of privacy, a need to insulate against climatic or environmental conditions, and undistinguished windows. And window coverings—striking in design as well as function—race to the rescue.

COVERINGS CONTRIBUTE MIGHTILY

The hanging of textiles dates from medieval times, when fabric was used to protect against drafty stone walls. This heavy-handed approach lasted well into the nineteenth century, when middle-class country homes boasted larger windows and with them wonderful window treatments, such as swags, jabots, cornices, and valances, decorated with colorful festoons, fringes, and tassels.

Modern window dressing often follows classical lines, updated with less formality, less voluminous styles, and more restraint, topped off with a touch of whimsy. Let the individual demands of each space, in terms of aesthetics and function, set the pace.

With the current trend toward a light, open feeling in room decor, window treatments as a design category have suffered undue criticism. Sometimes I think it's the antiseptically clinical connotation of the word "treatment" that sabotages even the best window coverings. "Window treatment"—the term lacks the warmth, beauty, versatility, softness, fluidity, and decoration that curtains, draperies, blinds, and shades can contribute.

Homeowners will say to me, "Now, I don't want anything to obscure the light. I love a sunny room; it's so warm, inviting, and cheerful."

I couldn't agree more. Just as hair frames a face, window treatments should frame the opening, not hang in front of it. Using fabrics that drape and hang well is like getting a good haircut that swishes back into place when you shake your head.

In fact, window coverings can perform little miracles, framing a pretty view or protecting privacy from curious neighbors. Fabric can accent the graceful lines of a window or disguise the lines of an awkward one. And with a careful and thoughtful wedding of fabric and style, window dressing has the power to alter the mood of a room—from casual warmth and softness to elegance and formality.

Let's take a look at fabric generally and then move on to how fabric works on windows.

CHOOSING AND EVALUATING FABRIC

Choosing fabrics is one of the most important elements of good design because fabric is so visible. Your draperies and window curtains and certainly the upholstery on your furniture—particularly if you choose a color or pattern—catch the eye immediately upon entering the space. Lighting, wall and ceiling paint, and even floor finish act more subliminally on the consciousness. Fabric commands attention.

Keep in mind when choosing fabrics that they perform functional as well as decorative tasks. In addition to enhancing the look of a room, fabric has the capacity to insulate against heat or cold and to absorb sound. An ultra-modern room with lots of steel and metal, illuminated by natural light from oversize, uncovered windows, will seem to clatter. Voices will sound harsh, music will shriek. No matter how interesting the look, you'll find the space unfriendly, uninhabitable.

Curtains and draperies; upholstered pieces such as sofas, chairs, loveseats, and chaises; and carpeting and wall hangings, equalize a room, contributing aesthetic appeal and usefulness. Never underestimate fabric. It is an outstanding decorating tool.

EMPLOY TACTILE AS WELL AS VISUAL SENSES

Before you choose a fabric, handle it. Feel it with your fingers. Touch it against your arms and legs, your face. Does it feel nice? Some people like it nubby; others prefer it silky. If it doesn't feel right to you, move on.

Crush it in your fist. Does it wrinkle? Pull on it a little. Does it stretch? Rub your hand back and forth across it. Does it seem to "catch?" If so, it might fuzz up or pill.

Before I decide on a fabric, I like to gather up a large piece in my hand and then crunch it, release it, then crunch it again. This shows me how the fabric will look when it's knotted, twisted, gathered, or folded into a drapery. Some fabrics drape better than others, as this tactile test will reveal.

Keep in mind that, like wall covering, if the fabric has a pattern, you will need to buy more material in order to match the pattern. A stripe is fairly easy to match, but random patterns may repeat only every 18 or even 36 inches. This is as critical in drapery making as in upholstering, where every cut calls for a pattern match.

You must always choose fabric "in place." If you're upholstering a chair, put the fabric sample (as large a sample as you can obtain) on the back of a chair, then on the seat. If you are choosing drapery material, hold it up against the wall. Don't choose a fabric for a vertical application (sofa or window treatment) from a horizontal plane (tabletop).

CHOOSE FABRIC FOR THE SETTING

Some fabrics are more appropriate for upholstered pieces than for windows; nevertheless, many choices in both categories make it possible to accommodate judgment and individuality with taste and discernment. No fabric can be all things to all people. A smooth or textured finish, a solid or a pattern, a casual or formal look—all are possible from among the myriad choices available.

How you balance form and function for the best and most lasting effect is another area in which you might want to consult an interior designer, whose eye for color, pattern and texture can weave fabric into a room in appropriate proportions.

In shopping for upholstery fabrics, consider tapestries for rich effects with excellent wearability, or denim, corduroy, flannel, canvas, ticking, herringbone, hopsacking, jacquard, twill, ottoman and tweed for informal rooms that will get hard use.

Chintz and satin provide a lovely, light look, but wear less well than many other fabrics; silk or cotton damask and velvet dress up a room and are surprisingly durable.

In evaluating cost, remember that price does not necessarily correspond to wearability. Tapestry is quite expensive and will last virtually forever; on the other hand, ticking is relatively inexpensive and will also last and last. Suit the fabric to the setting.

❖ *Formal settings.* To dress your windows, again consider the character of the room. If you are decorating a formal room, choose antique satin, brocade, damask, faille, or taffeta. Formal draperies must be lined in order to help fabrics hang with grace, to protect them from sun damage, water, and soiling, and to maintain a neutral and uniform appearance from the exterior view.

Two woven silks: a textured matelassé, inspired by a French botanical document, and woven picket fence, reflecting an ancient Japanese pattern.

Courtesy of Scalamandré

This cotton needlepoint fabric is an adaptation of the upholstery fabric found in the library at "The Elms" in Newport, Rhode Island.

Courtesy of Scalamandré

Another cotton needlepoint fabric adapted from upholstery fabric at "The Elms" in Newport, Rhode Island.

Courtesy of Scalamandré

An example of a silk and rayon strie damask stripe.

Courtesy of Scalamandré

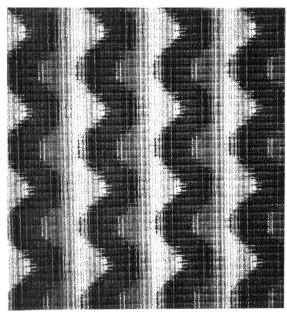

Linen and cotton boucle pattern.

Courtesy of Scalamandré

A cotton damask suitable for wallcovering, upholstery, and drapery, ca. 1910.

Courtesy of Scalamandré

Rich teal blue draperies may blend handsomely with the living room upholstery fabric and decorative pillows, while gold sets off the furniture in the dining room. But deep blue windows showing on one side of your house and gold windows on the other will destroy its exterior appeal. Draperies lined in an off-white sateen maintain a neutral tone outside with a stunningly bold interior effect.

❖ *Casual settings.* Truly casual cloths include gingham, calico, ticking, denim, and burlap—any of which make up well as cafe curtains or as other informal styles. Again, if deep colors show through the windows, line the curtains.

❖ *Traditional settings.* Somewhere between museum formal and family-room casual, you can choose Belgian linens, floral chintzes, polished cottons, or softly textured fabrics in solids, prints, and open weaves, lined if necessary.

CONSIDER PERFORMANCE

Window fabrics should be selected for performance as well as appearance, an approach that will help you narrow down the choices. Because a strong sun can damage color and fiber, fabrics intended for a southern exposure should be evaluated for sun resistance. If a window faces north, where it is subject to cold drafts, draperies can serve as added insulation. You will want to extend them beyond the window frame to shut out every bit of cold air. They should be lined, even interlined, for added protection.

In humid climates, window materials should be selected to resist mildew. In urban areas, they should be able to resist the corrosive soot and chemical fallout that penetrate even tightly closed windows.

If a curtain or drapery will be drawn back and forth on its rod frequently, it should be made of fabric strong enough to resist abrasion where it sweeps along the carpeting.

Washability is an important performance factor in a child's room, family room, kitchen, or bath. Look for a permanent-press or no-iron finish.

A timeless flowered fabric brightens an ivory silk textile.
Courtesy of Scalamandré

*Hand-worked trimmings reflect time-honored
production methods. Even with machines, the yarns
must still be guided by human hands*
Courtesy of Scalamandré

WINDOW TREATMENT OPTIONS

Here are some of the window-dressing options that can be adapted to
individual rooms:

❖ **Draperies.** Panels of heavyweight fabric hung in loose folds at the
sides of a window, usually to the floor. Draperies create a formal effect
in living rooms, and bedrooms, dining rooms.

❖ **Curtains.** Panels of lightweight fabric typically hung from rods,
usually to the windowsill. Most curtains are made of sheer fabrics, to
allow filtered light to enter a room. Curtains are appropriate in kitchens,

family rooms, and dens, also bedrooms and baths when used in conjunction with privacy shades or blinds.

❖ *Swags.* The ornamental use of fabric loops or drapes across a pole at the top of a window in a graceful arc. A swag is an easy look, appropriate in any less formal setting.

❖ *Jabots.* A word from old French meaning romantic throat. A jabot is an ornamental cascade of ruffles or frills down the front of a shirt, blouse, or dress. In terms of window dressing, a jabot can drape down from either side of a swag or valance. Jabots add a touch of formality to living room, dining room, and center hall window effects.

❖ *Austrian and balloon shades.* Fabric shades combine the effect of light, airy window curtains with the up-to-open–down-to-close feature of blinds and shades. Austrian shades gather into soft scallops when opened. Balloon shades, as the name suggests, work similarly but with a more billowy appearance. Pretty in bedrooms.

❖ *Roman shades.* These fabric shades work like Austrian and balloon shades, but draw up like an accordion, similar to slatted Venetian blinds. Often fashioned in textured fabrics, Roman shades are attractive additions in home libraries, home offices and dens, and in any contemporary, uncluttered space.

❖ *Valances and cornices.* Window toppers, such as valances and cornices, add a finishing touch to any window treatment. Fabric valances or wood cornice boards can be shaped across the bottom to complement any room style—from straight-edges in contemporary rooms to curves or arcs in period settings. Depending on the effect desired, they can range in depth from a narrow 8 inches to a dramatic 24 inches or more. Typically, window valances and cornices in average-size rooms are 18 inches. The deeper the topper, the more formal the effect.

BLINDS AND SHUTTERS

Fabric, because of its fluidity and versatility, is the most common window covering. Nevertheless, other materials adapt well to windows.

Blinds made of metal, wood, or vinyl, as well as fabric, provide a clean, crisp look whether used alone or with curtains or draperies. Blinds with horizontal slats pull up and down like shades; those with vertical slats open and close on a pull cord like draperies.

Slats come in widths—from 2 inches down to half-inch mini—and in scores of colors and wood tones.

As a category, blinds blend well into rooms, serving as low-profile workers that fit neatly inside a window frame, where they regulate the amount of light entering a room, disappear up and out of the way, or lower into place to maintain privacy.

Ready-made blinds, available in white or cream from good hardware stores or home centers, are quite inexpensive and come in many widths and lengths that cover most standard-size windows. They even come with their own matching cornices that hide the business end of the blind mechanism. Custom blinds can be contoured to fit nontraditional window shapes and sizes, and can be made up in a rainbow of colors.

Wood shutters, another option, work similarly to blinds, but present a heavier look. The frame of the shutter attaches to the inside of the window frame so that the shutter appears to be an extension of the window, particularly if the shutter wood is finished to match the wood of the frame. Louvers within the shutter framework operate like blinds to regulate light or shut it out completely.

The neat fit of shutters seems to cocoon a room—a nice feeling in a den, family room or bedroom.

*B*lairstyle Tips *on Attractive, Functional Window Treatments*

Today window treatments eschew the musty Victorian taste for heavy drapery. Large, exposed windows that let in lots of natural light have placed new demands on designers for new window configurations made from light fabrics that perform well.

❖ **Choose fabric in place.** If you're choosing drapery fabric, look at samples up against a wall.

❖ Aim for what I call "skimpy and uncontrived" window coverings that let materials soften and frame the view with fabrics that drape well.

❖ Anchor window dressing above the top and beyond the sides of the opening so that, when appropriate, all of the window can be exposed to let in as much natural light as possible.

❖ While I prefer draperies to curtains in most applications, lace and sheers can touch windowsills. For best effects, resist a lot of shirring with lace. A hint is plenty.

❖ Drapery hardware, too, is decorative as well as functional. Pretty rods with interesting finials at each end enhance a window treatment. You might consider covering an inexpensive pole with a piece of the drapery fabric, and then attaching your own decorative finials purchased from a good home center.

❖ When hanging simple cafe curtains, position the hanging rod down from the top of the window about a quarter of the way. This allows extra light to enter the room, enhances views, and still protects privacy.

❖ When hanging draperies, finish the look with valances and cornices. For drama and vertical lift in a large room, position the topper from the uppermost point of the window all the way to the ceiling.

❖ To add a feeling of width to an installation, position draperies to hang from the two side edges of the window to the corners of the wall. Over the window itself, hang sheers, shades, or, for added width, pleated shades or woven blinds with horizontal slats—providing the room is large enough to accommodate the added effect. You don't want a window treatment to overpower your room.

❖ When you have draperies custom made (or furniture reupholstered), be sure that all the fabric is ordered at the same time from the same dye lot. Slight variations in color occur in different dye lots. This is an important service a designer performs.

❖ Using the same fabrics, dress windows in the same room differently for visual interest. Similarly, in a case of mismatched windows, you can create visual uniformity by draping windows and adjacent walls to identical dimensions.

7

COLOR AND PATTERN

Color, more than any other design element, affects the mood and atmosphere of interior space. Its influence can calm and comfort, or introduce drama and excitement. Color communicates. We need to determine the design statement we want to make.

—JOSEPH HORAN, ASID
SAN FRANCISCO

The Practice of Prescribing Colors and Patterns in Appropriate Doses Makes Good Room Medicine with Value-Added Therapy

A JUDICIOUS MIX of colors and patterns defines the *feel* of space as clearly as any textured surface. A perfectly smooth wall with no hint of texture speaks one language in creamy vanilla, another in pale blue, and yet a third in sunny yellow. You need not put your hand on the wall or even approach it. The moment you enter the room, its color colors your mood.

Similarly, striped and plaid fabrics convey different messages than florals, and still other statements emanate from geometrics. Patterns can project seriousness or whimsy, classical motifs or playfulness. They can be bold or subtle and can appear in many forms—wall covering and flooring, groupings of art and collectibles, window dressings and furnishings—each delivering a different message, each playing on the inhabitant's mood, emotion, and outlook

Colors and patterns in appropriate doses are good room medicine with value-added therapy.

COLOR: FIRST QUESTION; LAST CONSIDERATION

"What color shall we paint the walls?" is one of the first questions new clients ask. In fact, color is one of the last considerations of the professional interior designer, who will first assess the space and determine goals, then plan how to meet those goals. Only after function and form are firmly established will the designer determine color, finish, and overall mood.

Any discussion in this area must first address the effect of light on color because even minute changes in the source and intensity of light affect the appearance of color.

❖ *Natural light* reveals colors in their truest form, because daylight contains equal parts of all colors of the spectrum: red, orange, yellow, green, blue, indigo, and violet. In darkness, on the other hand, there is no color. Shadings between the two light extremes—full-spectrum light (the presence of all colors) and black (the complete absence of color)—affect the hues transmitted back to the eye.

Pigment, which has the ability to absorb some colors and reflect others, gives objects color. An object that appears blue actually absorbs all the other colors *except* blue light. The unabsorbed light is reflected back to the eye, and the brain interprets the object as blue.

❖ *Artificial light* injects its own properties, creating subtle differences in hue. As a result, colors will appear differently during the day, when they are bathed in natural light, than at night, when illuminated by lamplight.

(Before)
The bare bones of an attic with the rafters clipped feels gargantuan, top heavy, and with little potential for charm.

(After)
This enormous room (50 feet long by 25 feet wide and 14 feet tall) easily handles multiple activities—pool table, state-of-the-art electronics and exercise equipment, comfortable seating bar, game table, and library—and design techniques handle the proportions.
Credits: interior designer Linda Blair; photographer Durston Saylor

Tudor-style leaded glass windows are still important architectural features, although modern insulation values are harder to achieve with older fenestration than with newer windows.
Credits: interior designer Anne Tarasoff; photographer Bill Rothschild

A dramatic wall of stationary glass doors is a good choice. For privacy and light control, draperies are on moveable rings.
Credits: interior designer Cynthia Kasper, ASID; photographer Tim Lee

The challenge of dressing closely aligned windows of different heights is met here by establishing one dramatic focal point with a pair of single tied-back panels and free-hanging drapery panels and simple lambricans throughout.

Credits: interior designer Linda Blair, ASID; photographer Kurt A. Dolnier

In a narrow foyer, theatrical drapery folds of several different fabrics create the backdrop for the recaimer and claim the area for a special activity.

Credits: interior designer Miriam Wohlberg; photographer Bill Rothschild

Simple white bamboo roll-up shades provide horizontal architecture and a background for the sofa and screen.
Credits: interior designer Mary Knackstedt, ASID; photographer Bill Rothschild

A library bay window is flanked by tall shutters topped by an original hand-worked felt cornice, all subtly colored to match the woodwork around the room.
Credits: interior designer Vince Lattuca; photographer Bill Rothschild

Muted surroundings—walls, window treatments, crown molding—create intimate dining, while the unusual colors in the area rug and seat cushions provide the tension a great room always has.

Credits: interior designer Joseph Braswell, ASID; photographer Norman McGrath

Red is always powerful. This sitting room/library works because the colors and objects are carefully balanced—rich walls, a mass of books, and a small-scale patterned carpet.

Credits: interior designer Michael A. Orsini, ASID; photographer Bill Rothschild

Light colors create a quiet style; brightly patterned draperies outline the windows, while dark woods and terra cotta finishes add balance.

Credits: interior designer Joseph P. Horan, ASID; photographer John Vaughan

Dark colors convey a sense of richness; the overall effect is of dark ceiling, floor, garden print fabric, and walls punctuated with the surprise of white moldings.

Credits: interior designer Joseph P. Horan, ASID; photographer John Vaughan

Quiet color and tiny pattern wrap the room, creating a cocoon effect, with punctuation from the larger-scale pattern on the bed for added contrast.
Credits: interior designer Teri Seidman, Allied Member ASID; photographer Bill Rothschild

Monochromatic schemes hold as up well as brightly colored ones. Restraint makes a big impact.
Credits: interior designer Cynthia Kasper ASID; photographer Tim Lee

(Before)
A forlorn jukebox, contrasting walls, and a dated orange and brown color scheme and window treatments are uninviting.

(After)
Color, proportion, and carefully placed furniture make a user-friendly room. Design solutions include starting the window treatment at the ceiling instead of a foot below, adding a "trompe l'oeil" (fool-the-eye) fireplace where there was none, and eliminating the dated technique of painting one wall a dark color by painting all walls one unifying soft color.
Credits: interior designer Linda Blair, ASID; photographer Durston Saylor

❖ *Candlelight,* the warmest of all light, enhances reds, oranges, and yellows. Similarly, cool colors, such as blue and green, become dull and lifeless in candlelight.

Let's look at an example. Many people choose to decorate kitchens and dining areas in green. Greens evoke visions of leafy vegetables and gardens, a natural complement to freshness and appetizing meals. The result, however, can be less successful than the imagery, primarily because of light.

At breakfast, a rising sun creates a pleasantly soft, restful hue. At lunch, when sun and colors appear in their full intensity, green enhances the lushness of a salad lunch, punctuated by ripe red tomatoes, yellow peppers, and orange carrots. These colors are close together on the color scale and so complement each other.

At dinner, however, after the sun has set, a greenish cast from fluorescent bulbs in the kitchen plays with the room's green tones, giving diners a sickly green color that deadens appetite and conversation.

Mood-enhancing candles on the table make matters worse; the fresh green tone comes across more like dishwater. You may find that your food tastes peculiar. Honest!

Incandescent light, with its slightly yellowish color, works better with green after dark, but still seems cool. Perhaps it's psychological, but hot food seems to cool faster in a green room. On the plus side, a room decorated with a green palette seems cool all summer long, even without an air conditioner. Hotels in tropical climates often decorate with lots of green.

As a general rule, fluorescent light tends to enhance cool colors and weaken warm colors; incandescent light, on the other hand, enhance warm colors and weakens cool ones.

COLOR AFFECTS MOOD

Now you're beginning to see how color affects mood. The ancient Oriental philosophy of *feng shui* points out the differences between yin rooms, which are darker and quieter, and yang rooms, which reflect light and liveliness. *Feng shui* balances these energies, fine-tuning them to create symmetry and accord. You can strive for symmetry and accord—and good *feng shui*—with color.

Public rooms (yang rooms), like living and dining rooms, libraries, and foyers, respond well to warm colors, such as reds and oranges and yellows, which elicit upbeat emotions. Red, which reminds us of heat and fire, can energize and stimulate. Yellow, like sunlight, raises our spirits. Translated into design, these colors stimulate conversation, intellectual activity, and laughter.

Bedrooms and bathrooms (yin rooms) are places of serenity, introspection, self-indulgence, and rest; they require calming coloration. If you enjoy a long, leisurely soak in a tub at the end of a long day, red would be a poor choice for your walls and accessories. Blues and greens, however, will calm you, soothe your frazzled nerves, and ease you to sleep.

What a bore, however, if everybody's living room were yellow and every dining room red. What about creativity, imagination, preference?

AN ENDLESS VARIETY OF COLORS

Rarely does any design call for pure-tone red—essentially the color an artist uses right from the tube. Pure colors lack subtlety and sophistication and, in most settings, would be much too intense, drawing the eye to the color exclusive of any other element in the room.

Just as an artist mixes pure colors with white or black to achieve compatible hues, the interior designer works with the Munsell color wheel, with its hundreds and hundreds of options, to arrive at a triad of shades based on colors you like that will work together to achieve desirable effects.

All of us learned in elementary school that red mixed with yellow makes orange. But, suppose you use more yellow than red, or you lighten it with a little white, or tone it down with some blue or green, or infuse it with some purple? Now an individual and personal-preference effect is beginning to take shape.

By the same token, two identical colors look different against different neighboring colors. Gray will look darker on a white background than on black. Red will look stronger against green than against orange, because red and green are contrasting, while the red and orange are homogeneous.

WORK WITH COLORS YOU LIKE

Attention to personal color preference accounts for the most successful rooms. A young couple once told me that they wait all year for those seven or eight days in autumn when the leaves on the huge maple tree in their front yard turn bright yellow/gold—just before they're released for the season in a final blaze of glory. For those few days, while their whole house is bathed in a golden glow, the couple arise early and hurry downstairs to watch the gorgeous transformation from first light to brilliant gold. If the phenomenon occurs over a weekend, they plan a brunch for friends to share the warmth.

Nothing we do can duplicate exactly the color splendors that nature provides, yet an approximation can awaken pleasant experiences. In the case of the "maple-tree couple," they chose a color range from pale yellow to amber for the three rooms most affected by the annual autumn ritual—a decision that not only brought to mind an enjoyable and much anticipated experience throughout the year, but also served to enlarge the space.

In the center hall, the wallpaper blends garnet and gold, adding luster to the Shaker-style hallway table and providing direction to the flanking rooms and up the stairway, where they display photographs of their beloved maple tree in all seasons.

In the living room to the right, walls painted a creamy ivory represent glorious sunshine and a cheerful mood. To the left of the center hall, soft gold, tempered with a touch of warm, Tuscany brown creates a happy and congenial dining atmosphere.

COLOR SCHEMES THAT RELATE AND CONTRAST

Typically, color schemes are monochromatic, homogeneous, or contrasting. Here again, let personal preference be your guide. Picture the color spectrum as a wheel, starting with red and moving through red/orange to orange, from orange through orange/yellow to yellow, from yellow through yellow/green to green, from green through green/blue to blue, from blue through blue/indigo to indigo, from indigo through indigo/violet to violet, and finally from violet through violet/red to red.

One person's idea of elegance might be a series of monochromatic tones like ivory and beige (created from a mixture of yellow, red and white) carried through the walls, carpeting, and furnishings. Another might see this choice as lifeless, preferring instead homogeneous colors composed of several neighboring hues on the color wheel—say, a blending of blue, green, and violet shades.

In a contrasting scheme, colors are chosen for their distance from each other, not their proximity, on the color wheel—say, yellow and violet, which are directly opposite. Here, shades of both primary hues can be picked up in patterned throw pillows or wallpaper borders, table skirts, or other decorative elements that introduce color. Care must be taken to ease the eye from one color to the other in intervening steps, lest the effect become harsh or garish.

For the most part, lighter shades wear better on the senses; darker tones tend to become wearying. Deep, bold color can be exhausting and hard to live with. As a rule, whether you like lighter or darker colors, create a palette made up of a series of three or four shades that are closely connected, highlighted with occasional accents. Charles Grebmeier, ASID, a San Francisco designer, suggests black.

"Black," he says, "is the place where the eye and the soul tend to rest most easily. Black, then, can become the subtle thread that ties a room together."

THE COLOR WHEEL: A PRACTICAL APPLICATION

For her home in New York State's Hamptons resort area on Long Island, a summer resident wanted to preserve beach tones throughout the house. She chose buff for the walls, ivory on trim and ceilings, and used a textured, sand-toned upholstery in the seating areas, a combination that reminded her of a windswept beach, she said.

For beds, tables, and storage, she choose a light, driftwood-toned maple.

As an accent color with the sands and ivories, she opted for terra-cotta—a warm blending of red, orange, and yellow (neighbors on the color wheel) with a touch of black—carried through in gradual increments in kitchen floor tile, area rugs and bedspreads. The scheme worked particularly well in the bedrooms, providing a cheerful mode during the day and maintaining serenity once the bed coverings were removed and stored for the night.

She carried through the color scheme on the outside as well with tan/beige shutters against an ivory/white house, and finished off the look with masses of white, gold, and red-orange flowers in the window boxes.

Pattern—To Evaluate Pattern, Step Back

HUNDREDS OF COLOR possibilities lay the foundation for tens of thousands of patterns, an endless variety of centuries-old shapes and forms from around the world. Ethnicity, religious beliefs, celebrations, discoveries, designs, animals, plants, elements and minerals, stories and

Woven bouclé from The Mission Collection.
Courtesy of Scalamandré

folk tales, free-form abstractions—all suggest categories of patterns available to the home decorator interested in introducing an important visual element into an overall color design scheme.

Like color, pattern contributes to mood and ambiance within a room from the moment of entry. You can feel the effect of a pattern without touching it; you feel the rhythm, the depth, the enrichment. Bold and dramatic, or subtle and understated, pattern is a powerful design tool that adds personality and visual interest to space.

Pattern is everywhere. Designers introduce it through textiles— window treatments, upholstery, accent pillows—and to a lesser extent through flooring, carpeting, wallcovering, and art.

Interior designers call the assessment of pattern effectiveness and appropriateness a "reading." How a pattern reads explains how its colors and design relate, balance, and harmonize with other elements in a room.

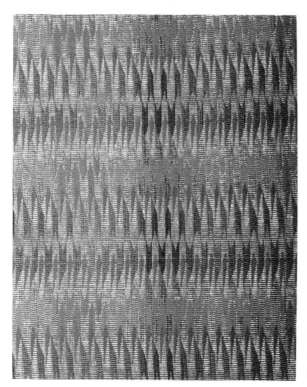

A gobelin textile reminiscent of Indian arrow feathers.

Courtesy of Scalamandré

"Good Medicine" matelassé, a pattern of the Plateau Indians, was thought to bring good health and luck with its use.

Courtesy of Scalamandré

COMPATIBILITY IS THE KEY
TO COLOR AND PATTERN

Growing up, you may remember your mother saying, "Don't mix stripes and plaids," or admonishing your father for putting on a foulard tie with a pinstripe suit. "Too much pattern," she would declare. "Too busy."

Today, we know that a patterned tie and a patterned shirt *can* work together if the patterns are harmonious and the colors compatible. Making that judgment—whether or not two elements are simpatico—is one of the most challenging aspects of interior design, and often the reason that color and pattern are uppermost on a client's mind.

Homeowners can address the physical properties of a room: the height of the walls, the square footage of the floor, the amount of natural

A priest's chasuble, woven in the eighteenth century, inspired this hand-printed reduction.

Courtesy of Scalamandré

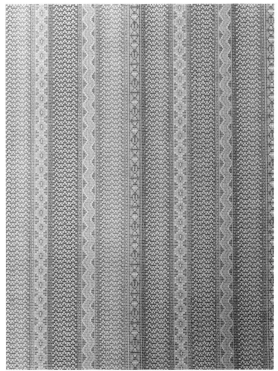

Inspired by a Pomo Indian basket, this textile reflects the art of weaving.

Courtesy of Scalamandré

light available at various times of the day. With these elements carefully plotted, a workable design plan begins to emerge.

But subjective decisions—Is this color a better choice than that color? Does this print go with that stripe?—can stymie the most brilliant mind unless the intelligence reflects a fine designer's eye and technique. What goes with what requires an advanced degree in sophistication and self-confidence with a minor in risk taking.

SEEING IS BELIEVING

At first thought, a floral print sofa would appear to fight with the seats of a pair of chairs upholstered in a stripe. Yet by assessing the width of the stripe and evaluating the way similar colors in the floral print relate, the patterns will complement each other. Careful study of size, scale, type, and style of patterns—plus colors and color relationships in each— create harmonious results. To devise such a plan requires large textile and carpeting samples, ample-size paint chips—and flair.

One of the tricks to incorporating pattern into design is to choose the dominant color and repeat it in a solid elsewhere in the room. Don't pick an inconsequential color within the pattern. Instead, take a step back and see which color appears to jump forward. That's the one to match or reinforce within the space.

Texture adds another value to pattern, and with so many fabric options available today, you can enrich any design plan with texture, from formal to casual. Choose a silk brocade or tapestry print for classical appeal, a velvet or velour for formal rooms, a cotton corduroy, twill, or woven for family rooms and dens. In the home office, decorate with needlepoint, tweed, or flannel to soften hard-edge technology with homespun detailing.

Texture provides depth, a three-dimensional tactile quality that influences design. You may not feel comfortable sitting on a nubby fabric, or particularly surefooted walking across a textured rug. But picking up a tapestry throw pillow or hanging a textured rug or interesting imported fabric on a wall lends importance.

Heavy woven tapestries offer solid images reminiscent of Tudor or Jacobean decor. There's nothing lighthearted about these patterns and fabrics unless it's their ease of maintenance. Cottons and chintzes, on the other hand, offer brightness and high contrast, often with flowers abounding. Like most natural fibers, cotton is surprisingly durable and easy to live with and care for.

I have clients who are so satisfied with the look and durability of a chintz pattern I chose for them eight years ago that they are reupholstering the furniture with fabric exactly like the original. Now, that's an endorsement.

*B*lairstyle Tips
on Choosing Colors

❖ **Natural color rhythms reminiscent of the earth create familiar, comfortable surroundings. Following nature's lead, choose darker hues for flooring (the earth), medium colors in the middle (trees and flowers), and pale tones at the top (the sky). Add a gentle touch of pale blue to a white ceiling.**

❖ **Use color to unify space. The same color carpeting in a center hall and the living and dining rooms ties the three rooms together, particularly if they are visible from one to the other. Furnishings and complementary colors individual to each room provide character and personality.**

❖ **As a rule, colors close in hue work better together. Let gray bridge the step between black and white; an ivory/beige/taupe combination is more attractive and easier on the eye than brown with white.**

❖ **Avoid overly matched schemes. Neutral shades can work in several rooms, but limit more colorful groupings to single rooms. A dramatic living room or dining room with intense color should stand alone; choose homogeneous or monochromatic colors in adjoining areas.**

❖ **Similarly, limit accents. Too many accents arranged helter-skelter lack connection. Better to arrange several pillows in one corner of the sofa than to pop an accent pillow on every seat in the room.**

❖ **Choose colors associated with pleasant experiences and colors that you like. If you dislike pale aqua, you shouldn't use it, no matter how popular it seems to be. In fact, avoid trends at all cost because they are costly in the long run.**

❖ Bright colors visible from the crib in the nursery fascinate and amuse babies. Consider framed art or a trompe l'oeil mural. For children who like to play in their rooms, decorate with a color they like. Ask them.

Blue often is a childhood favorite. Choose several hues, ranging from light to medium, breaking up the singularity with yellow/green accents. Blue in children's rooms—not for boys only, by the way—provides a bright, primary color that tots like, without encouraging hyperactivity.

❖ Remember that color sets the tone of space and can influence activities. Use color to control mood and energize atmosphere.

*B*lairstyle Tips on Decorating with Pattern

❖ Let patterns blend rather than oppose. Choose designs, colors, and patterns by standing back from the fabric to determine the dominant relationships.

❖ Choose textiles by examining them *in position*. If you are picking drapery fabric, choose from samples placed vertically against a wall, not flat on a table. If you are looking for chair fabric, look at the samples on a chair seat and against a chair back. Patterns appear different, and provide different effects, in different positions.

❖ Patterns create color and shape relationships within themselves that should be reinforced elsewhere in the room. You want a handsome pattern to be noticed, not to stick out like a sore thumb.

❖ A well-designed Oriental rug is the most outstanding of all fiber patterns and often the most important design element. As such, a fine Oriental is appropriate in any room, any time, with any decor, performing functional duty on the floor or serving as an artistic wall hanging. Determine the dominant hues, and choose furnishings and colors accordingly.

❖ Hardwood floors, wainscotted or paneled walls, the grid of ceramic tile, and marble also contribute pattern to a room, without inhibiting the use of other patterned elements.

❖ Historic patterns, frequently replicated by major manufacturers, will continue to withstand the test of time. Newer patterns, particularly those that border on the bizarre, may be attention-getting but quickly grow tiresome.

8
SOFT
FURNISHINGS

As we approach the twenty-first century, technology is zooming in on us, almost in a menacing way. It is reassuring to know that textiles, which have been woven by man since the dawn of history, are once again of major importance. Fabrics provide one of the richest sources of human comfort, enhancing all interior environments.

—ROBERT HERRING,
VICE PRESIDENT, F. SCHUMACHER & CO.
INDUSTRY FOUNDATION MEMBER, ASID
NEW YORK CITY

Sit Before You Buy

IT'S HARD TO BELIEVE, but comfortable upholstered furniture (soft furniture as opposed to wood tables, chairs, and case-goods pieces) as we know it today has been in use for little more than a hundred years. Upholstered benches, known as divans or banquettes, appeared in the eighteenth century, but the notion of slipping into an easy chair or stretching out on a comfortable sofa is relatively recent.

The middle class, life-style, leisure time, and creature comforts—concepts as foreign to the early settlers as the New World itself—have crept slowly into the vocabulary and the mainstream. And naturally, house furnishings to indulge a middle-class life-style with leisure time and creature comforts proved equally long in coming.

By the middle of the nineteenth century, however, country houses were filled with comfortable upholstered furniture, many in styles that remain today with remarkably little change. Typically, these pieces, symbolic of new money, were found in huge halls called great rooms, located near the front door, where farmers, social callers, bailiffs, and the occasional politician were received.

This idea of "clubby, casual association" clings to upholstered furniture today. People still refer to overstuffed chairs as "club chairs."

HEALTHY FURNITURE

At the same time, houses also boasted formal drawing rooms or parlors, where smaller, more formally styled upholstered pieces rested. The furnishings may have rested, but the people did not. Formal drawing rooms with their stiff chairs and settees set on spindly legs, hardly invited relaxation. Clearly, this furniture kept the uptight upright, or the upright uptight. In either case, visitors rarely outstayed their welcome.

Although traditional period furniture remained popular through the turn of the century, a new modern style began to develop. From about 1910, furniture designers began to use other materials, such as steel and aluminum and glass. They supplemented these elements with plywood and common lumber frames that were easy to mass-produce and easy to camouflage with pretty fabric coverings.

Today, more generous proportions create a more healthful receptacle for the body, keeping it supported yet relaxed. Why more people don't take advantage of this well-designed comfort is a puzzle to me. I'm always amazed at how many men haven't a single comfortable reading chair in their homes.

Women may adore playing Scarlet O'Hara on a delicate settee or filling the living room with period antiques, but those styles don't respond well to curling up with a good book. Purchase well-constructed upholstered pieces for medicinal purposes as much as for style and function.

GOOD CONSTRUCTION
MEANS GOOD VALUE

The value of a sofa lies in its construction. Choose a sofa the way you choose friends. Don't be taken in by a pretty face; it's what's inside that

An antique recamier infuses a sense of history throughout the room.

Credits: interior designer Linda Blair, ASID; photographer Fred Payton

counts. Look for character and depth. That's where you'll find the quality.

Sit before you buy. Take off your coat and sit a while. Popping up and down on one sofa here and another one there doesn't allow you to collect enough information to make an informed judgment.

"OUR HOME" FOCUSES ON SOFT FURNISHINGS

Two of my first four appearances on the Lifetime Cable Television Network's "Our Home" show involved soft furnishings. To some degree that indicates their importance.

On my first appearance, a segment on sofa buying, I took viewers to one of my favorite upholstery factories and showed them how quality furniture is put together—from the wood frame to the fabric covering. Then we went to a large New York City showroom, where the show's host sat on, bounced on, jumped on, lay down on, and finally decided

Linda Blair Design Inc.
Interior design
(914) 472-5690
1 Chase Road, Scarsdale, N.Y. 10583

With a sectional or simple sofa, a comfortable chair placed at a right angle permits easy conversation. Make the chair a swivel if a television is nearby.

Credits: interior designer Linda Blair ASID; renderer Robert So

on a sofa for his apartment, with viewers and the host learning together how to go about it.

In preparation for a newspaper article for the *New York Post* Women's Editor, Kathy Bishop, about buying a sofa at retail, I enlisted the help of my elderly mother, my 5-foot, 2-inch daughter, and my over-6-foot husband—three people with very different priorities for comfortable seating—for a field test to see what consumers were being told by sofa salespeople. The results of our test were quite surprising and not entirely satisfactory.

PERSPECTIVE VIEW OF
FAMILY ROOM
LINDA BLAIR DESIGN INC.

Linda Blair Design Inc.
interior design
(914) 472-5690
1 Chase Road, Scarsdale, N.Y. 10583

A FIELD TEST

While all of us were treated nicely in the stores, overall we found the sales help woefully uninformed. When we said we were interested in buying a sofa, they asked us, "What color?" When we asked about construction, they told us about the fabric or had to refer to a fact sheet. When we asked about the warranty, not one knew exactly what the warranty actually covered.

"Probably fabric," one said. "Maybe construction," another thought. "Wear and tear," someone else suggested.

You should ask for the department manager or buyer, and get this information in writing.

While my husband liked the trendy loose, floppy feel and the leather look, my mother had trouble getting into and out of these kinds of seating. She did better with more traditional styles that offer more support.

My daughter had the hardest time finding a good fit. Many of the sofas on the market today were too deep for her. Her legs dangled, and her back started to hurt after a relatively short time sitting. Her youth and casual style seemed to draw her to the trendy, plushy styles, but she confessed she found them rather uncomfortable.

I had a similar experience. Even good brand names with floppy styling lacked support. The quality was there—8-way hand-tied construction or nonsag frames, but the filling was too soft for ease in getting in and out. Besides, a too-soft filling has no memory; you'll spend too much time plumping pillows.

At a furniture discount store, I found the prices appealing but the samples short on support. Many styles offered large pillows as a backing instead of built-in sofa cushions with pillows in front. With this type of construction, you lean back a long way to find support.

Bottom line (no pun intended): look hard, sit a while, and ask lots of questions. Be a tough customer.

The sofa-buying segment, put together with the benefit of my field test, was very successful, largely because the situation is so relevant. At some time or another, everyone needs to buy a sofa, and in fact few people understand how to go about it and why some sofas are so much more expensive than others.

A BEDTIME STORY

My next appearance on "Our Home" explained how to buy a mattress. For this segment, we had several well-known, brand-name manufacturers deliver their products to the studio, and we invited a couple from the studio audience to try them out.

They lay down, rolled over, and assumed typical sleep positions. This prompted lots of chuckling, but viewers learned to identify the elements that separate poor mattresses from quality ones. The test was how comfortable your body feels the next morning. In the end, they realized that bargain mattresses are no bargains.

In addition to a sofa-buying and mattress-buying how-to, I've also included in this section a few tips on how to buy a down comforter. This accessory truly belongs in the category of soft furnishings because it represents a considerable financial investment. You should know what you're buying.

*B*lairstyle Tips
for Identifying Quality Sofa Construction

❖ Lift up one end of the piece. If it's heavy, chances are it's well made. That may seem like a superficial test, yet it's easy to do and will help you eliminate a poor piece right away. If a piece is too easy to lift, the manufacturer probably has skimped on materials in the construction process.

❖ When you sit down, do you hear creaking sounds or squeaks, or does the piece feel wobbly? These noises are indications of poorly made furniture. With solid construction, you'll feel and hear only solid comfort.

❖ If possible, look at the exposed wood on the underside of the piece. Unraveling fabric edges, streams of glue that have dripped and dried, knots in the lumber, or nailed joints are signs of inferior quality.

❖ The best frames are crafted from kiln-dried hardwood with minimal knots. The best woods are birch, maple, poplar, and sycamore. Avoid particleboard and very soft or very hard woods. Joints should be doweled or screwed, and then stapled for reinforcement or carefully glued. Legs must be attached securely to the frame with corner blocks for extra strength and stability.

❖ Examine the springs and look for 8-way coil springs that are hand-tied to one another on a base of steel, with up to three layers of padding over the springs. Newer methods include "nonsag construction" with doweled or glued corner blocks. Staples should be used as extra reinforcement only.

❖ Cushions should yield when you sit on them yet provide good body support. Soft, resilient polyester or down, wrapped around an inner core of dense foam, is the best filling. Cushions shouldn't be overly large; when you sit back, your legs should bend easily and your feet should touch the floor. Look for cushions shaped like gentle mounds. A rounded rather than flat cushion not only looks more comfortable, it is. Trust your eye here.

❖ Look for good tailoring represented by straight seams without puckers or loose threads, soft but well made.

❖ Look at the fabric *under* the cushions, too. This area, called the deck, should match the upperside.

❖ Remember, a high price doesn't always mean high quality or durability. An inferior piece may be covered in an expensive fabric that drives up the price. However, low price often reflects poor quality.

❖ When you choose fabric, feel is as important as look. Touch it against your arms and legs, even your face. Does it feel nice? Does it wrinkle? Does it stretch? Does it seem to "catch?" Remember, the softer the fabric, the softer the seating.

❖ Always choose fabric "in place." Put the sample (as large as you can obtain) on the back of the sofa, then on the seat. Don't choose a fabric for a vertical application (sofa or chair) from a horizontal plane (tabletop).

❖ If you order a piece of soft furniture, you may have to wait weeks or perhaps months. Upholstery manufacturers may have to wait for your fabric selection to be delivered from the fabric mill. Please be patient. Good craftsmanship takes time.

❖ Before you buy a new piece of furniture, consider recovering an old one, particularly if you are lucky enough to have an older sofa or chair of superior quality. A good workroom can modify and update an older piece, giving the 1970s quality a 1990s look.

*B*lairstyle Tips *on Buying a Mattress*

The following guidelines, suggested by the International Sleep Products Association in Alexandria, Virginia, will help you make your most important health-beneficial soft furnishings purchase—a mattress and box spring set. This can be costly but worth the price for top quality. Don't stint. Your back will forgive any financial extravagance.

❖ *Comfort.* Gone are the days when a mattress had to be hard as a board to be good for you. In fact, these days chiropractors and doctors seldom advise inserting a board. On the other hand, if you feel as if you're sleeping in a hammock, the mattress is too soft. You'll sleep best when your bed helps you feel cradled in comfort—cozy and secure.

❖ *Support.* Correct support is the essential ingredient for a healthy body. A good mattress and foundation will support your body gently at all points and keep your spine in the same shape as that of a person with good standing posture.

Pay special attention to the heaviest parts: your shoulders, hips, and lower back. If there's too little support, you can develop back pain, but if the mattress is too rigid you can experience uncomfortable pressure.

A word about "firm." Don't rely on product labels to tell you which mattress will give you the right support. One manufacturer's firm may feel harder than another's extra firm. The only way to find out if the support is right is to lie down and try.

❖ *Durability.* The quality of the materials used and how they're put together determine how long a mattress and foundation will provide the comfort and support you bought them for. The best assurance of good performance over time is to buy the best-quality sleep set you can afford.

Don't expect a set of bedding to last forever. After 8 to 10 years of nightly use, even the best bedding no longer will provide the best comfort and support.

❖ *Space.* Cramped quarters can turn sleeping into a nightly wrestling match. A healthy sleeper moves anywhere from 40 to 60 times a night, including some dozen full-body turns. You need freedom of motion while you sleep and to help you relax while getting to sleep.

If you sleep with a partner, you may want to select a queen- or king-size mattress set. Both are wider and also several inches longer than the standard double. It might surprise you to learn that a double bed offers each sleeper only 27 inches—as much space as a has baby in a crib.

❖ *The innerspring.* The most widely purchased type of bedding uses the support of tempered steel coils in a variety of configurations. Layers of upholstery provide insulation and cushioning between your body and the coils.

There should be more than 300 coils in the full-size version of the model you're considering (more than 375 in a queen and more than 450 in a king). Also, check the thickness of the wire gauge. The lower the number, the more durable the wire (13 is thicker than 16).

❖ *Foam.* Foam mattresses offer a wide choice of "feels." They can be made of a solid core or of several layers of different types of foam laminated together. The newer, high-resilience polyurethanes and the more traditional latex (synthetic rubber) are among the highest-performance foams. Be sure the foam in the mattress you select has a minimum density of 2 pounds per cubic foot. In general, the higher that number, the better the foam.

❖ *Flotation.* Waterbeds are available in two basic styles: The hardside type is a vinyl water mattress, liner, and heater contained in a rigid frame; the newer softside style looks much like the familiar mattress/box spring combination. Both types offer a range of feels from "full motion" to "waveless." Like electric blankets, waterbeds now have separate controls for heat.

❖ *Foundation.* A good foundation (box spring) is as important as a good mattress. It acts much like a large shock absorber, taking a lot of the nightly wear and tear. It also contributes to comfort and support.

Don't put a new mattress on an old foundation. Purchase them together because they are designed to work together.

❖ *Purchase.* When shopping for a mattress, take your partner. Wear comfortable clothing and shoes you can remove easily when testing the mattress. Lie down and stay down; you can't judge support and comfort by sitting on an edge or by lying down for a few seconds. Don't be shy. Shop for the best value, not the lowest price. You can always find bargain bedding at low prices, but it's no bargain if you must sacrifice a good night's sleep or your health.

*B*lairstyle Tips on How to Buy a Down Comforter

Buying a down comforter doesn't have to be a wild goose chase, but it should be treated as an important investment that will deliver many years of warmth and pleasure. A down comforter can be the focal point of your bedroom, where you cocoon yourself for a third of your life.

❖ *Try it on.* Buying a down comforter is like buying clothes: You need to know how the fabric feels and how it "fits" around you. Let a down comforter envelop you before you buy, and be sure you like it because a good one should last 10 years or more.

❖ *Note the stitching.* Closed stitching forms a series of sealed "boxes," keeping the down in place.

❖ *Look for baffles.* Baffles are little walls of fabric that create space where down can loft and provide more insulation. Baffles eliminate cold spots caused by sewn-through stitching.

❖ *Examine the fill power indicated on the label.* Fill power is the primary way to measure the quality of a down comforter. Fill power of 500 to 550 is good, and 600 to 700 is worth the extra investment. Fill power of 800 is quite luxurious.

❖ *Insist on pure cotton comfort.* Cotton, densely woven, is the best way to keep down in and is also the most comfortable fabric to sleep on. To keep down clusters from flying around the room, the cotton should have a thread count of at least 230 threads per inch. The higher, the better. The duvet will still need a cover to protect it. If you're allergic, choose cotton or synthetic fillings over down.

❖ *Check the warranty.* A long warranty is a sure sign of a quality comforter. Read the warranty carefully so you will know what it covers.

❖ *Be earth-friendly.* Down is a natural by-product of the world's poultry industry and is fully biodegradable, making it an environmentally correct bedfellow. Down can be folded into your garden as fertilizer when bedding reaches the end of its serviceability.

9
HARD FURNITURE

A cabinet with doors or drawers gives a room substance, warmth, and mystery. As repositories for possessions, closed cabinets safeguard the items deemed most meaningful to their owners. To me, a room without a closed cabinet is dull and antiseptic. It lacks excitement.

—JOHN ELMO, FASID
NEW YORK CITY

Good Design Promotes Good Health: Dangling Legs Are as Bad as Dangling Participles

MAKE FURNITURE BUYING an ongoing source of pleasure and satisfaction, a lifelong pursuit of adding and repositioning that corresponds to life-style, interest, and mood.

Take the small storage chest next to a sewing machine, the one that comes in so handy through the years that mothers work to keep up (or down) with daughters' hemlines. When the daughters are tending their own hems, the same little wooden chest—with the patina earned from many years of service—can be retired from active duty, living out its dotage as a quiet side table in the living room. Or maybe it will be pressed into service once again beside a daughter's sewing machine.

Or take our Aunt Elsie's mahogany Governor Winthrop desk, which she purchased in 1942 for $89. This cherished piece, with its flip-down writing surface, ample drawers, wonderful small cubbies, simple good lines, and fine workmanship, was first housed in her living room. Today it has a value of about $3,900, and it is an important bedroom piece in our home, awaiting its role somewhere else with the next generation.

Such is the life of a fine piece of furniture, carefully chosen for its charm and quality, an investment that continually contributes beauty and value.

So, too, with other furniture. An apartment-sized dining table becomes a work table in tomorrow's family room. Newlywed living room pieces furnish the den in a couple's first house. An investment in furniture for the long haul is a good investment and one that provides excellent value. That's recycling of the finest order.

CAN YOU AFFORD IT?

Is quality furniture more expensive? Yes, of course. It costs more because it's worth more; it's worth more because it will serve better, hold up better, and look better longer. Selecting furniture that reflects taste and quality requires a lot of time, patience, and a sense of appropriateness to form and function.

Probably you shouldn't buy the first piece that catches your eye, because furniture buying is a learning experience. You need to talk to people, to look not only on top but underneath at the construction and the joints, to run your hand over the wood, to slide the drawers in and out. Only by comparison will you begin to see the differences that indicate quality.

When one of my clients was house hunting, she passed up the first house she was shown, a wonderful English Tudor that would have suited her family excellently. How was she to know? She hadn't seen anything else, and she figured that what she had just seen was only the beginning of wonders yet to come. She didn't bid on it, and rued the day as the procession of inappropriate properties lengthened.

Happily, a Colonial on larger property in a better school district came along. The family has been very happy. Similarly, you may pass up excellent pieces of furniture at first, but others will surface. And by then you will have developed the skills and confidence necessary to recognize them.

GET PROFESSIONAL HELP

Because many pieces of fine furniture represent a considerable investment in time and money, you would do well to seek help with this search. An interior designer is trained to select furniture with all five senses: to feel a fine piece of wood, to see that legs are properly braced, to hear the strength of solid wood, to smell the natural oil of a well maintained piece, and to "taste" or savor the history of a piece of furniture that has withstood time—in essence, to recognize furniture of lasting value

How to recognize and buy quality hard (case goods) furniture—tables, chests, desks—is what this chapter is about. We'll also give some thought to how furniture is placed for maximum visual and functional

Chippendale-style furnishings always set an elegant tone. Note the built-in cabnetry, which always adds visual interest and additional storage

Credits: interior designer Marilyn H. Rose; photographer Bill Rothschild

At one time, every home had a Windsor chair. How pleasant to see it again, this time at a gateleg dining table. Note the side table and host chair are in different styles and woods.

Credits: interior designers Josef Pricci and Eaton Square Antiques; photographer Bill Rothschild

appeal. Soft furniture—sofas, upholstered chairs, bedding—are discussed in connection with fabrics in Chapter 8.

Only when the Industrial Revolution introduced large-scale factory production in Europe and America did we enter the age of the furniture set, or more pompously, the suite. Is it heresy to blame the Industrial Revolution for the sad state of interior decoration by suite or set?

Sometimes I think we might be better off, in terms of furniture at least, if the assembly line never had developed. Imagine, all furniture

Saarinen chairs and a custom table are offset by the clean lines of the custom storage wall, reminiscent of the simplicity of Arts and Crafts furnishings.

Credits: interior designer Linda Blair, ASID; photographer John T. Hill

beautifully handcrafted by artisans who care deeply about their work, who imbue each piece with their love. That would preclude the boring banality of the bedroom suite of headboard, dresser, chest, and bedside tables—all matching; the dining room suite of table, four side chairs, two armchairs, sideboard, and hutch—all matching; the living room suite of sofa and two side chairs—all matching.

Some modern furnishings, made from established manufacturers like John Stuart, Witticomb, Hitchcock, Baker, Kittinger, and Smith & Watson, retain their value. But most are easily discarded with no loss to the rooms they inhabited, to the consumers who purchased them, or to the offspring who needn't experience any familial obligation to them.

A TRADITION OF INDIVIDUAL PIECES

In the early years of this country, young people furnished their homes—no matter how grand or modest—with pieces inherited from their parents. In nearly every American home, the family sat down to dinner at a dining table that had belonged to mother's mother and on chairs that had once belonged to father's aunt.

In each case, individual pieces represented a kind of dowry, a sense of family history, a place of honor. The chair at the head of the table was quite different from its counterpart at the foot. Each side chair offered a different grace. Eclectic, yes, but joined by tradition, quality, and value. And as a statement of interior design, wonderful!

ANTIQUES MEASURE UP

It's the thrill of the hunt that inspires the antiquer. Shops, flea markets, antique shows, and auctions all have their special allure and personality, and you never know what you'll find. In the beginning, it's better to look generally rather than specifically. When you need pieces for every room in your home or apartment, does it really matter if you find the perfect chest of drawers before you find the perfect dining room table? I think not. So keep an open mind.

Collect styles of furniture as you would collect books or *objet d'art.* Our rich legacy of furniture styles encompasses many countries over many centuries. What you choose reveals what you've seen, what you value, who you are.

Take advantage of the spectrum of wood furniture—an intricately carved case piece made of mahogany, walnut, or satinwood, either burled or highly polished, endows a formal living room with variety and character. Or, choose a rough-hewn pine, oak, or maple kitchen table with utilitarian, Shaker-style chairs for a blending of history in a more casual manner.

Little by little, as your rooms begin to take shape, you can browse with specific fill-in pieces in mind. One of my clients has been looking for a small, antique chest of "just the right size," she says, for about five years. "When I see it, I'll know it," she declares. Frankly, I don't think she'll ever settle on any chest, because then she'll have nothing left to search for and no compelling reason to browse the shops, the shows, and the flea markets. A chest of "just the right size" gives her purpose.

THE AUCTION EXPERIENCE

Buying at auction is quite another matter. Here, real know-how is required. You've heard about people getting caught up in auction fever— bidding more than they can afford or more than a piece is worth—just to win it. Make up your mind that you may have to forfeit something you really love, maybe because those bidding against you have auction fever.

You'll learn a great deal by listening to a professional, by watching how someone knowledgeable examines a piece at the viewing prior to the actual bidding, weighing construction details against condition of the piece, evaluating a piece of furniture's representation of its period, its intrinsic beauty, its modern-day practicality.

With experience, you will be able to estimate an opening bid and, more important, to set a top price above which you absolutely will not bid—and stick to it.

IN SEARCH OF QUALITY

We all know about tire-kicking car buyers. Well, you'd better not try that test on a piece of fine furniture, or you'll own it faster than you can say "hardwood veneer." There are more appropriate methods for assessing quality furniture.

❖ *Wood.* The term *solid wood* means that the piece is made of maple, oak, or cherry all through, not with a thin veneer of fine wood glued to plywood or particleboard. Solid wood implies strength and durability as well as beauty. Solid wood furniture is more expensive than veneered pieces—and worth it.

Among the hardwoods, mahogany, cherry, oak, walnut, and maple are the most commonly used for furniture. They are from slow-growing deciduous trees, valued for their rich grains and strength.

The so-called soft woods, such as pine, cedar, redwood, and fir, come from faster-growing evergreens suitable for more utilitarian purposes, generally not fine furniture.

❖ *Joints.* How pieces are joined at the corners determines their ability to hold up under stress. A better joining method produces better-quality furniture. Furniture components can be secured with staples, nails, screws, joints, and glue, usually more than one method per piece. Staples, the weakest connection, appear on budget furniture; nails are somewhat better, followed by joints and glue, which appears on nearly all connections.

- *Butt joints,* where two boards come together like a house of cards, are weak.

- *Miter joints,* where components meet at corners on an angle, fit better than butt joints but need reinforcing with nails or screws.

- *Tongue-and-groove construction* joins two boards that meet side by side, with a strip from one slipping into a groove on the other.

- *Dovetail joints* are among the strongest and an indication of quality furniture. In this method, seen particularly on drawers, components fit together like interlocking fingertips.

- *Dowel joints,* also strong, connect pieces with dowels imbedded into both components.

- *Mortise and tenon construction* calls for a sizable projection at the end of one board fitting exactly into a cutout in the opposing board. This method, too, indicates strength because it distributes stress over a wide area.

❖ *Finish.* Let your eye and your sense of touch guide you. Quality furniture will be finished lovingly—sanded, glazed, waxed and buffed so that the surface is hard, smooth, and even. Poor-quality furniture will be sealed with a layer of polyurethane.

A fine cabinetmaker uses care and skill; commercial pieces often show sloppy finishes. It's harder and harder to find beautiful finishes on finely crafted pieces, but don't let the difficulty force you into buying inferior items.

❖ *Construction.* Open and close drawers and cabinet doors. Look for center or side glides and drawer stops that prevent drawers from pulling all the way out. Run your hand over the inside of the drawers to make sure the bottoms and sides have been sanded and sealed.

See that cabinet doors fit into their grooves and close properly. Examine the hinges for strength. Look for dovetail or doweled joints, well-turned legs, and finished back panels, which provide more flexibility in placing the piece of furniture in a room. Sometimes you don't want to back furniture up against a wall.

CONSIDER THE SPACE AND THE FUNCTION

Before you purchase any piece of furniture, recheck the specifications of your original plan. A gorgeous dining table loses its allure quickly when it's squeezed into a small dining space. An antique side table, despite its charm and colorful history, if intimidated by an oversize couch can throw a whole room out of proportion.

Select furniture for its space and for its function. All furniture serves a purpose: chairs, stools, beds, and sofas are articles for rest; tables and desks, articles for work; bureaus, bookcases and cabinets, articles for storage; stoves, lamps, and fans, articles for environment control. How these articles are placed in an area introduces the element of organization. That they also contribute elegance, grace, ambiance, and beauty enhances quality of life.

So, a small two-drawer bureau placed in a bedroom with an inadequate closet is a wasteful investment *for that space.* You're smarter to keep looking until you find a four-drawer chest or, better still, a tall, narrow, seven-drawer chest with sizable storage capability as well as vertical interest.

Assess the furniture you have to determine what you need. In the paragraphs that follow, let me suggest some hard furnishings and arrangements to consider.

❖ *In the living room,* think about a handsome low chest of drawers, particularly one with beautiful hardware, which can double as an excellent side table next to or behind a sofa, or as a stand-alone piece against a wall. In either location, the surface of the chest can accommodate a lamp, a collection of vases or framed photographs. The drawers provide storage, which is always an advantage.

A tall secretary makes a stunning focal point in any room and, at the same time, provides a writing space for creative work or mundane tasks like bill paying. Secretaries are desirable pieces of furniture and can be costly but well worth it. In good condition, they hold their value through generations, often selling later for much more than their original price.

On the subject of tall pieces, no single item has the power to add drama to space or to break the eye's arc from floor to ceiling quite like a screen. Available in many styles—Oriental, wood, fabric covered, glass, bamboo, flat-topped, arc-topped—screens are hard-working elements. Like a tall plant, they help bring furniture into proportion and serve as a wonderful backdrop to art, a reading chair, or upholstered pieces. Moveable feasts for the eye, screens can hide office areas, exercise equipment or, the doorway to a kitchen. Or they can make an area cozy, creating an intimate niche for conversation or activity.

In the apartment where I grew up, we had an antique mirrored French screen angled near the door to the kitchen. Although every piece of furniture was carefully chosen, the image of the screen has stayed with me through the years. More than any other, it is the one item that summons up my childhood.

COFFEE TABLES AND END TABLES

Coffee tables, whether iron, glass, lacquered, wrapped, or wood, are serviceable pieces and good accents for rooms. They can be 23 to 27 inches high—like English tea tables—to hold books, plants, vases, and collectible objects, or hassock-height—16 to 18 inches—to hold a beverage tray or a stack of magazines.

To flank sofas, choose tables (not matching ones, please) that are high enough to reach without stretching or straining your arm (25 to 30 inches is about right). Absolute heights are difficult to standardize because sofa seating is so variable. Also, you tend to sit lower on a softer, more cushy sofa seat, which then calls for a higher side table. Since you don't want to lift yourself halfway off the sofa to pick up your reading glasses.

By the way, many people find a too-low seat uncomfortable. For this reason, I always include at least two straight-backed chairs, often with a higher table "suitable for tea," in addition to a traditional sofa-with-club-chairs arrangement in every living room I design.

Choose lamps for the tables that will add to ambient light while providing task light for close-up work, like reading or sewing. As with end tables, choose different styles for design interest, but be sure the lamps are the same height with the shades in place. The only proper way to choose new shades, by the way, is to bring the lamps with you to the lampshade store. Where height is important, bring both lamps to avoid mistakes.

❖ *In the dining room,* the table is the most important piece of furniture. Take your time in choosing one. With so many options, how you serve and how you entertain will influence your choice.

Realizing that her present Parsons-style dining table without leaves could no longer accommodate married children and the prospect of grandchildren, one homeowner purchased a 1930s double-pedestal table with three leaves—on her 30th wedding anniversary.

"It's true, most of my friends are downsizing at this point in their lives," she observed, "but I like to make family dinners here, and I want everyone to be comfortable. If my family is growing, I'm happy to make provisions."

The table she selected not only will accommodate her growing family but will become a family heirloom—forever mother's table, to be loved and cherished, evocative of wonderful memories of family gatherings. The dining room table is without a doubt a wonderful investment of incalculable value.

Standard height for a dining room table is 28 to 30 inches. I always feel that a higher rather than lower table helps people slide their legs under and cross them if they choose. On the other hand, reaching a too-high table causes upper-body discomfort. Factor in chair height— usually 17 to 19 inches from floor to seat—and size of apron below table top. It's best to test. Don't choose in a vacuum; bring the chairs to the table and try them out.

Round tables are hospitable. They create intimacy and encourage conversation. At a round table, no one feels isolated at one end or at the "head" taking charge.

True, a round table is more difficult to extend. Leaves make a round into an oval, but the curved "ends" make comfortable seating more difficult. Think about how you entertain . . . and how many diners you typically invite to your table.

A word about pedestal tables: Support from the center rather than at the corners keeps table legs from interfering with diners' comfort. At dinner parties, I always seem to get a chair with the leg and end up straddling it between mine. It's unfortunate, undignified, uncomfortable, and totally unnecessary.

The best solution in the dining room: an antique pedestal table (check all the usual sources, plus consignment shops, where my friend purchased her double-pedestal table complete with three leaves) paired with chairs built with good, lasting support.

CHAIRS FOR HEALTH, STYLE, AND COMFORT

Select for style and comfort. Rare tropical woods make stunning chairs, but undermine ecological conservation. Instead, choose more common woods, beautifully designed and lovingly finished.

Chairs affect health, and good interior designers promote good health as well as good design and good value. Comfort, a catchall concept, encompasses an understanding of orthopedic science. Ideally, the height of the seat should be adjusted so that both feet can be placed firmly on the floor while the thighs are horizontal. When your legs dangle, blood circulation is impeded, pressure increases on your thighs, calves increase in size, and the temperature of your toes drops. When selecting chairs, keep this in mind: dangling legs are worse than dangling participles.

I like the look and feel of an eclectic mix of chairs around a fine dining table—upholstered his and hers chairs, with wood chairs for guests—for an elegant and interesting effect.

❖ *In family rooms,* spend the money for furniture that can take a beating. With more women working, with later hours and less time, the family room is today's equivalent of the Colonial hearth, bringing the whole family together for television, computer games, music, and conversation. Kids want to eat on the floor, adults want trays on the coffee table, but all hands want comfort, no-fuss easy-care decor, and sturdy furniture.

❖ *For the children,* remember that kids aren't gentle. They're small and they're cute and endearing (some of them!), but they wreck things. Furniture particularly. Give your child a drawer, and before you know it, it'll be filled up with slimy rocks and rotting tree bark. Even dainty little girls, who tiptoe upstairs to make afternoon tea parties for their dolls, spill and crumble and smear.

Kids cram things in drawers and closets and under beds. They pile their belongings on top of leftover peanut butter and jelly sandwiches, and crayons run amuck. Even when they're falling-down tired and sent to bed, they don't just slip in. It's an attack plan—a running start from the hallway and a giant leap battering-ram style against the headboard. Night after night after night.

Kid-test furniture before you buy. Bring your darlings along and let them take a flying leap into the bed to see how the unit responds to abuse. Let them slide the bureau and desk drawers in and out a dozen or so times to make sure they work easily and stay on track.

Have them sit at the desk, stand on the chair, and lean against the bookcase to make sure it doesn't wobble. And be sure to inspect the joints and hardware for quality workmanship and durability. Any salesperson who looks askance may have something to hide.

You can opt for high-density particleboard covered with a laminate top or wood veneer. Personally, though, I like solid wood construction.

Wood-mode kitchen cabinetry forms hanging and fold-up storage and a trundle bed for a child's room.

Credits: interior designer Karen Berkemeyer; photographer Tim Lee

Strategically placed storage units create, define, and control space.

Credits: interior designer and renderer Robert So

It'll last through several children and serve as accent pieces elsewhere in the house once the little ones have outgrown it.

❖ *In any room of the house,* consider a rocking chair for comfort, relaxation, and, like Proust's tea and madeleines, a remembrance of things past.

*B*lairstyle Tips *on Selecting Hard Furniture*

❖ Don't feel compelled to buy the first piece of furniture you see that seems appropriate for the space and function. You need to shop and compare in order to recognize a truly fine piece. Hard furniture can last several lifetimes; you can take a little time in order to select carefully.

❖ Avoid matching sets. You'll achieve a more interesting look and a more satisfying room with a variety of woods and styles.

❖ Seek professional advice before buying antique furniture, particularly at auctions. Always attend the auction preview to get a good look at a piece that interests you—inside the drawers, at the joints and connections; on the back and underside.

❖ Occasionally, position wood furniture somewhat away from walls to create the perception that it is "floating" in space. This technique endows each piece with importance and makes walls recede in significance.

❖ In large spaces, group furniture pieces into cozy conversation areas, each with its own small tables and chests. This nesting approach humanizes large areas, augmenting comfortability.

10

KITCHENS
AND
BATHS

Sometimes people mistakenly relegate kitchen design to the back burner, so to speak, concentrating instead on a home's showplaces, like the living and dining rooms. Kitchens and baths—spaces used most continually— must be as comfortable, attractive, and workable as any in the home.
—SARAH BOYER JENKINS, ASID
WASHINGTON, DC

Kitchens Are for Living and, Oh Yes, for Cooking

IN LIFE'S DAILY drama, the kitchen has taken center stage. Today's kitchen is the hub, the center, the very heart of the house.

It was not ever thus.

The Victorians, for example, considered the kitchen a second-class citizen—a barren, antiseptically clean, and purely functional necessity relegated to a location as far from the master's view as possible. In Parisian bourgeois houses, kitchens were placed off the courtyard, with limited access to other rooms. However, the kitchen has progressed considerably in stature in the 300 years since the Renaissance, when it housed dogs and chickens as well as household help in the lower level of the house.

It took the Dutch to endow the kitchen with respect, feminizing the home around the seventeenth century and thereby launching one of the most important trends in domestic interior design—the kitchen as a center of family activity.

Practical by nature, Dutch women, regardless of wealth or social position, ran the household with three or fewer servants, so the mistress of the house typically hung out her own laundry and cooked many of the family's meals. Lacking the conveniences we now take for granted, these women did the best they could with what they had. And elevating the kitchen—physically as well as functionally—seemed a logical step. Household servants may have had no voice in kitchen design, but certainly the lady of the house did.

American women typically took an active role in running the house and, like the Dutch, performed a great many ritual household tasks. In so doing, they recognized the importance of a centrally located room, a command center, from which to direct domestic activity.

KITCHENS MOVE BEYOND MEAL PREPARATION

Whether your domicile is a modest house or a sprawling affair measured in acreage, chances are you spend a fair amount of time in your kitchen. Make it work for you. And remember, while the occasional gourmet cook may surface from time to time, meal preparation is not always the kitchen's main function.

I am a perfect example of that phenomenon. My dream is a complete kitchen renovation. I think about it every time I walk into my kitchen. I can see how the space will look, how it will open to a beautiful great room, where my growing family can mix, mingle, and relax.

And yet, except for holidays when the whole family pitches in, I haven't cooked in years. Nevertheless, someday I want to have this wonderful kitchen because a kitchen can be so much more than the sum of its parts. My new kitchen and the proposed family room are where I hope I'll visit with my grandchildren.

Think about it. You plan a social get-together or a party with friends or family, and with virtually a whole house open to your guests, you find them congregating in the kitchen. When the kitchen is attractive as well

as user-friendly, kitchen dinner parties provide the evening's entertainment as well as repast.

Every kitchen—in addition to its built-in cabinetry and shelving—has a built-in agenda. Food is love. Pleasure and generosity go hand in hand with the rituals of preparing and serving food.

THE KITCHEN: AN EXCELLENT INVESTMENT

Remember, too, that the kitchen can be the nexus of today's smart house—designed to accommodate television, VCR and CD player, phone, fax, Rolodex, and computer, as well as breadbakers, pasta machines, coffee grinders, espresso/cappuccino makers, trash compactors, intercoms, water purification systems, and built-in grills. Today's

All white gloss cabinets, white walls and trim, high-traffic flooring, mirrored backsplashes, and granite counters make this kitchen a breeze to maintain and, thanks to newly installed windows, with a grand view as well.

Credits: interior designer Linda Blair, ASID; photographer Kurt A. Dolnier

Deep mahogany offers the perfect pitch for solid surface flooring, similar to countertops. Lots of storage and a commodious island make the kitchen space function well for large-scale entertaining.

Credits: interior designer Michael A. Orsini, ASID; photographer Bill Rothschild

kitchen should provide a pleasing environment that will comfortably accommodate all the activity—and bring a handsome return on your investment.

In planning your kitchen, consider the following elements:

- A serviceable table is a must. Invest in an old wood table. The patina that comes with age and use adds to the charm of a kitchen, recalls the hearth of yore, and sends out a message that welcomes family and guests to the hub of the house. A long, narrow country table, if you have the room, can handle several activities at the same time, plus as many guests as your children invite.

- For countertops and islands, consider a high-pressure decorative laminate, like Formica, for durability and easy maintenance; solid-surface tops like Corian for cleanability and repairability; ceramic tile for beauty and versatility; marble or granite for elegance. Butcher block or maple stripe, as well as stainless steel and tempered glass, are good countertop insert materials for chopping and cutting.

- Build in plenty of cabinets, drawers, and other storage areas. Counters with pullout shelves offer easy access to cookware, small appliances, canned goods, and spices.

- A kitchen island is its own paradise—architecturally interesting and wonderfully functional—providing charm as well as additional storage, counter, and work space. Islands can be equipped with additional cooktops or sinks; many are double-leveled to separate work areas.

- Give thought to recycling, too, and set aside room (be sure it's enough) to accommodate bins for various categories of plastics, paper, glass, and metals.

- Floors, counters, and cabinets, made of wood or laminate, should be built to withstand rough use and, at today's prices, to last.

- Bay windows and skylights are nice features for bringing outside light in. Sliding glass doors let light in and provide easy access to a deck or patio for outdoor entertaining.

- Personalize your kitchen, just as you would any other room in the house. Display your collections of tinware, glass, and knick-knacks; decorate with unusual and personal items.

GET PROFESSIONAL HELP

Your new kitchen, with its special requirements for up-to-the-minute technology, up-to-the-inch space planning, and warmth and charm, may call for the special expertise of a professional. Kitchen dealers mainly want to sell cabinetry. Seek an interior designer who can plan your kitchen for best possible function and life-style enjoyment.

A new kitchen isn't an overnight job. Allow about four to six weeks for planning and at least two months from the time the first work crew appears at your door.

Costs vary tremendously, of course, depending on materials, labor rates in your area, and the extent of your kitchen project. Are you gutting your kitchen—taking it down to the beams and rafters—or can you get by with a simple facelift—a few nips and tucks here and there?

Whatever the cost, I guarantee this: Virtually every minute you spend in your new kitchen you will enjoy, and virtually every penny you spend on your new kitchen you will recoup.

Baths: The Modern Bathroom Should Provide Some Degree of Private Indulgence

HISTORICALLY, THE BATH provided pleasure as well as hygiene. Egyptians bathed to purify themselves before daily prayers; Greeks believed in the fortifying powers of cold showers; and Romans saw the bath as a public meeting place. To this day, many swear by the healing powers of mineral-rich waters and mud baths.

Back on terra firma—and after a quick reality check—where in a typically jam-packed 24-hour schedule does an ordinary career-focused, child-rearing, volunteer-minded mortal find the time for this entitlement, its therapeutic and restorative powers notwithstanding?

Must the bath be strictly business? A simple repository for toothpaste, Band-Aids, and shaving cream? A hasty shower with a deodorant soap? A quick flush before heading out the door?

Let's hope not. The modern bathroom should provide some private indulgence, however brief. While there may not be time to linger in the tub, certainly we can make even hurried visits to the bath comfortable.

What's wrong with a bit of luxury? Let your bath be a marriage of ancient ritual and modern technology, a unique sanctuary that offers unbounded design possibilities. You deserve it. We all do.

Small space is visually enhanced by a large expanse of mirror and the use of the same elegant stone on the counter, walls, and floor.

Credits: interior designer Susan Mellis, Allied Member ASID; photographer Robert Buchanan

PERIOD LOOK; INDULGENT CONVENIENCES

One of my clients asked me to create a modern, indulgent bathroom in her turn-of-the-century home, without compromising its period authenticity. It was a challenge I eagerly accepted.

First, I opened the common wall between the master bedroom and a guest room, envisioning the two rooms as the new master suite. I reapportioned the newfound space into two sections and reclaimed it as a master dressing area and a master bathroom.

The dressing area works particularly well, housing the client's pro-digious collection of designer clothing and shoes; it also serves as a prelude to the connecting bathroom. I covered the dressing area ceiling with a floral-patterned paper that I continued down onto the walls about 12 inches, anchoring it with a period-appropriate wood molding all around.

The newly created canopy preserves the turn-of-the-century charm of the house, while the storage closets and built-ins below, with their traditional detailing, provide ample room for current wardrobe and future additions.

In the bathroom, I installed luxuries never dreamed possible by the original owners: a mix of nonslip tile and marble in a soft watercolor print; recessed ambient and task lighting, including a heat lamp over the tub; large mirrors everywhere; and rich, all-brass shelves and hardware.

An oversize whirlpool tub with wide ledges for displays of collect-ibles lifts the bathroom above the ordinary. A coordinating toilet, bidet, banded-edge vanity installation with plenty of drawer space, and recessed storage niches for bath accessories round out the facilities. For colors, I chose a hint of Colonial green with a peach hue for warmth and authenticity.

QUALITY IS LASTING

Once I designed an all-marble bathroom in a fashionable New York City Park Avenue apartment, using thick slabs of it on the walls, floors, and tub surround. It was a very expensive installation at the time and also very beautiful. But, because I insisted on the finest materials and work-manship, the bathroom is as beautiful today as it was then.

Modern bathroom design employs materials never dreamed possi-ble years ago. Wood, marble, and ceramic tile with nonskid properties have been found to adapt well, even to harsh treatment by water and steam. These natural, high-quality products retain their looks and their value, providing many years of excellent service.

In fact, bathrooms have taken on a whole new look these days. Exercise equipment, clothes closets, greenhouses, and casual furniture are turning up with some regularity.

Linda Blair Design Inc.
Interior design
(914) 472-5690
1 Chase Road, Scarsdale, N.Y. 10583

A FAVORITE ROOM

A friend of mine and her husband just returned from visiting their daughter and son-in-law in Dallas, where everything is big. They had a wonderful time, she reported, describing the couple's huge house in great detail.

"My favorite room has the most wonderfully comfortable chaise and side chairs, and the television is just the right height for leaning back and relaxing," she said. "Sometimes the four of us and the two children with their toys and the dog would spend an entire evening there."

"What a nice, cozy feeling in the family room," I offered.

"Oh, no," she said. "The master bathroom."

This perspective shows placement of the tile, tile murals, and painted paneling that end up as a stylish pair of his and her bathrooms.

Credits: interior designer Linda Blair, ASID; renderer Robert So

*B*lairstyle Tips
on Evaluating Your Kitchen

A recipe for a great kitchen requires attention to these key ingredients: storage cabinets, work surfaces, backsplashes, appliances, state-of-the-art gadgetry with multiple options, flooring, and lighting. How does your kitchen measure up?

❖ STORAGE CABINETS

- Are the drawers, hinges, and hardware in good working order?
- Is there enough cabinet shelf space?
- Do you have tall pantry storage in the kitchen?
- Is the cabinet finish in good shape?
- What about space for recyclables?
- Do the doors open wide?

❖ WORK SURFACES

- Is there enough counter space?
- Is the countertop material easy to clean?
- Is the countertop in good shape?
- Are the counters conveniently located—where you need them?
- Does the color reflect your taste?

❖ FIXTURES AND APPLIANCES

- Is the sink in the right spot, near the center of activity?
- Can your sink be enhanced by a small, adjacent vegetable sink or a one-piece faucet with spray attachment?
- Is your microwave easy to get at?
- Is the refrigerator/freezer large enough for the family, and located near the preparation and eating areas?
- Are the oven and cooktop well located for ease of use? Remember, the oven (if not attached to the cooktop) is the least used appliance in the kitchen, and should be located out of the way but not blocking a doorway when the door is dropped.
- Is the cooking surface easy to clean, all burners working?

❖ MECHANICS

- Do you have task lighting above the countertop?

- Is there an attractive light fixture in the eating area?

- Are there light switches where you need them, and plenty of outlets? I always build in many more outlets than I think a client will need because sooner or later, they're needed.

- Are the plumbing pipes leak-free?

- Do you have a good ventilation system in the cooking center?

❖ GENERAL ORIENTATION

- How's the view?

- How's the traffic pattern? Do household activities get in the cook's way?

- How does the kitchen relate to adjacent rooms? Is it central, with multiple access points?

- Is the kitchen well lighted, safe?

*B*lairstyle Tips *for Indulgent Bathrooms*

❖ Just as I recommend against sets and suites and everything matching in other rooms in the house, I do so in the bathroom as well. Incorporate different finishes, hardware, and product lines. Use white and cream fixtures in the same bath.

❖ In planning your bathroom, remember that new features like water pressure restrictors in the new ecologically correct three-gallon toilets (unlike the old ones that use seven gallons per flush) are now required by most state building codes. Watch for new shapes and finishes in faucets; choose levers instead of knobs for easier use, and install acrylic tubs with relaxing motorized flows of water.

❖ Seek out shower heads (with water restrictors) with water pulse options for amazing body sensations.

❖ Choose clear glass shower doors for a sense of openness. Consider half-panels instead of whole doors—believe it or not, they do the job!

❖ For additional luxury, install heated towel bars to make the simple act of drying off a sensual experience.

❖ Build in as much storage as possible for towels and toiletries. Also, create space for a telephone and television, so that you can escape yet never be out of touch.

❖ And add enough outlets to accommodate all the new appliances you'll want.

11
TECHNOLOGY

Technology is advancing every second, presenting new and exciting ways to communicate and produce. Never before have we been so in touch. Interior design must respond to the new demands with accommodation and flexibility.
—ROSALYN CAMA, ASID
NEW HAVEN

You Never Have Enough Closets, Money, or Outlets

YOU DON'T HAVE to be a computer genius to recognize the enormous effect of technology on our daily lives. Just count the number of clocks and clock radios you reset every spring and fall, at the onset and end of Daylight Saving Time.

Only a few years ago, the semiannual changing of the clocks involved maybe six instruments: one in each bedroom, one in the kitchen, another on the living room mantle, plus a wrist watch. Nowadays, the hour you save each fall easily gets eaten up in the act of resetting.

Think about it. In addition to the usual, you've got VCR clocks, television clocks, computer clocks, automobile clocks, and telephone clocks. There are clocks that govern your lawn sprinkler system, security alarm system, HVAC system, outdoor perimeter lighting, and indoor room lighting. Clocks control your coffee pot, crockpot, electric stove, and microwave. There's even a clock that will release water to your plants when you're away for the weekend.

The multitude of clocks is symptomatic of a society preoccupied with and dependent on new technology to perform more tasks better and faster than ever before.

TECHNOLOGY SUPPORTS
THE DESIGNER'S GOALS

Welcome, I say, to any and all things that make life easier, more convenient, more comfortable, more orderly and, as a result, more attractive. Technology, a boon to humanity, also supports the goals of good interior design—convenience, comfort, organization, and look.

However, as gadgets and techno-products proliferate, the need to plan becomes increasingly critical. Where are you going to put this equipment? And how do you space it out to accommodate function as well as form? And hide the wiring?

Thanks to the microchip, fiber optics, and other developments, office capability is increasing as the equipment to perform office tasks is getting smaller. Remember when businesses needed entire rooms to house their computer systems? Today you can call for an appointment on your cellular phone, compose a confirmation memo on your laptop, and fax it to the client—all from your briefcase.

And that's just the beginning. Printers come pocket-size, CD-ROMs and modems can fit into the palm of your hand, and an entire encyclopedia will compress onto a $4\frac{1}{2}$-inch disk. In today's office, copy, answering, and fax machines are providing more services than an entire secretarial pool.

So, do you line up units on a counter, build them into cabinetry, or stack them on a rollaway that rolls away? These are the basic design decisions that result from thoughtful and intelligent planning that keeps you from creating rooms devoid of charm, history, or character.

FAX IT OVER, MODEM IT IN

The business landscape is changing dramatically. Today, you are just as likely to find a corporate headquarters in your neighbor's house or apartment as you are in a downtown office building.

As large companies restructure and downsize, more and more people are choosing to work from home. Recent studies reveal about 47 million people in the United States who have foregone the expense, commute, crowds, inflexibility, and stress that accompany working in

This Texas-size home bathing spa features a fireplace, garden, lounge, and high-tech luxuries.

Credits: interior designer Barbara Schlattman, ASID; photographer Hickey-Rubertson

an office in favor of at-home work. Thanks to growing acceptance, at-home workers need no longer feel they also have to forego cachet or posh, comfortable surroundings.

Not only has the home office come into its own, its easy, at-home style is influencing a redesign of corporate America. People are calling on designers to create professional efficiency in home office settings, and homey touches in typical skyscraper offices.

There's nothing new about working at home. Most professionals, in fact, bring work home to get a jump on tomorrow's agenda. The news is that modern technology creates an atmosphere of flexibility that permits corporate executives as well as individual proprietors to run profitable businesses entirely from home.

Home offices are out of the closet; wood paneling, an angled desk with ample counter space, and lots of cabinets to store equipment and supplies balance well with the fireplace inside and the scenery beyond.

Credits: interior designer Marilyn H. Rose; photographer Bill Rothschild

SMALL AND POWERFUL

In the past, the Internal Revenue Service determined that a desk, filing cabinet, and telephone constituted a workable office—and a legitimate deduction. However, today's at-home workers aren't content to settle for just those bare essentials. And why should they? Everything they need to conduct business in style can be accommodated in a relatively small area.

Typically, you can earmark perfectly acceptable space for a home office—complete with all necessary equipment and accouterments—without sacrificing family living quarters. A spare bedroom, maid's room, side porch or sunroom, attic or basement storage area—even an armoire or closet—can be converted into an attractive, efficient work area.

In addition to housing and accessibility of office machinery, you must address proper lighting (overall ambient as well as task directed) desk and chair ergonomics for comfort and health, electrical wiring and placement of outlets, temperature and ventilation, privacy, storage, conferencing capability, barrier-free design, counter space and work areas, and a host of details that make an enormous difference in the look as well as the function of a home office.

Every home worker has individual requirements and preferences; a home office should address equipment needs as well as the working style of the user. If you like to pound your computer while listening to rock music, plan for it; design it in; create a place for the components. Stacking stereo equipment "around" in a small space, particularly, will have you drowning in clutter faster than you can say "compute@home.com."

In designing a workable home office, you must consider amenities beyond technology:

- Plan plenty of vertical and lateral storage to avoid clutter now and to accommodate future expansion.

- Be sure you can hide thick computer cables and that you have a place to deposit ever-thickening piles of daily mail.

- Take advantage of natural light without creating glare on your computer screen, and select colors that complement the environment, reflecting your informal yet professional surroundings.

A HOME-OFFICE ADDITION

The first step in building a home office is to assess needs, space availability, working routine, and family considerations. For one professional planner, this realistic analysis resulted in a 750-square-foot addition to his house that would accommodate his practice, a waiting room with private office, plus a clerical area and, as long as he was building on, an exercise room that he and his wife could use.

Clean lines and lots of open space generate a feeling of spaciousness in the new mini-wing, while details like a cathedral window, a circular staircase, and a partial two-story ceiling provide architectural and visual interest.

Large windows on the southern and eastern exposures welcome the morning light and completely eliminate glare from the afternoon sun. Ambient light from energy-efficient, fluorescent fixtures recessed into the ceiling, supplemented with high-intensity track lighting for tasks, maintains a comfortable light level throughout the day with plenty of reserves for close up work.

As a result of good planning, the office houses, without crowding, three computers, dot matrix and laser printers, two copy machines, blueprint copier, fax modem, answering machine, postage meter, and stereo system. Vertical and lateral files, shelving, carpeting, and even a coat closet complete the picture.

Result: a roomy yet cost-efficient work space with all the technological amenities to make the handling of large projects do-able and small projects still profitable.

RECLAIM EXISTING SPACE

Ideally in any design project, you want a no-holds-barred budget and a large, pristine space. More commonly, you get a limited budget, a less-than-perfect area, and a mandate to create an intelligent, functional, aesthetically pleasing environment. This is the time to roll up your sleeves and call on all your skills.

One of my clients decided a few years ago to establish an independent practice in her home and, at the same time, to make a place where her husband, too, could take advantage of office amenities. A double-duty work arrangement, where both could be productive, made good practical and financial sense.

First we addressed the givens: two nonrelated his/hers business activities in one space; a small, lower-level room with little design interest; a low, seven-foot ceiling; no storage whatsoever; and one "he-refuses-to-part-with-it" rolltop desk.

Then we factored in the needs: a conference area to be used commonly; huge storage capability; and an outside entrance with an accessible closet for office overflow as well as family and client outerwear.

As the primary user, she would command the lion's share of the space. Yet he needed to feel comfortable in his work area, not hemmed in.

HIS, HERS, AND OURS

We established a roomy alcove for him with a simple bookcase that separated his territory from hers. The unit also gave him the storage he needed while adding architectural interest to the total concept. In the process, he got 45 square feet of breathing room plus 12 linear feet of storage files topped by another 12 feet of shelf space for books, plants, and collectibles—a touch that harmonizes well with his rolltop desk. We hung light-filtering pleated shades from the ceiling for privacy, for softness, and to convey a sense of height.

She, on the other hand, wanted to create an upbeat, contemporary feeling to convey the idea of cutting-edge, up-to-the-minute information that her clients expect. At the same time, she wanted the space to be comfortable and anxiety easing—an environment that would build trust.

Solution: two 20-foot rows of shelving, plus another 20 feet of work surface supported by one 35-inch and two 42-inch lateral storage files. The unit, which wraps around two walls and offers plenty of countertop for desk work and electronic equipment, is made of top-quality steel for ease of operation.

We laminated and then edged the cabinetry in wood for aesthetics and easy care. Considering the size of the unit as well as snowballing home-office technology, we invested in plenty of electrical strips to accommodate expansion. The client laughed when she saw them all. Three years later, she's still laughing—about how much money she saved and inconvenience she avoided by planning for the future in the present.

FINISHING DETAILS

To finish the job, we used built-in, wall-hugging furniture that makes her space appear larger and also opens up the center of the room for conferencing. We chose four sturdy matching swivel chairs—two stationed at the conference table and two to roll easily from the countertop for extra seating. We upholstered them in an inviting neutral-toned textured nylon for durability and paired them with a natural-wood round table with a bullnose rim to relax the hard-edged business end of the room.

To mesh the two work areas, we coupled perimeter under-soffit task lamps—that tend to enlarge space—with nonglare recessed ceiling lights for overall illumination and ambiance. A warm vanilla wall color throughout softens the linear momentum and weds the two work areas.

To add to the illusion of size and depth, we used low, horizontal shelves that stretch a room and lift the ceiling. Even the artwork simulates spaciousness: two park scenes that bring the outside in combat the underground feeling while adding perspective and depth.

Start to finish, the double-feature home office took only about five and a half weeks to complete, largely because highly motivated clients were willing to address details, accept advice, and make decisions. Cooperation produced a finished product that was sound, satisfying, comfortable, and reflective of both their tastes and their business requirements.

Having made an economical decision to renovate rather than build, they could more easily afford top-quality products throughout, a judgment that has rewarded them handsomely in terms of growth, maintenance, and durability.

LIVING WITH TECHNOLOGY

The entertainment value of technology is captivating. Television and television games, recording and playback capability, sound systems, and giant viewing screens fit nicely along walls, where you can tuck cables and wires neatly behind large cabinetry and components.

Problems surface, however, when you try to interface electronics with generic space. Site-specific areas like media rooms and home

A large TV screen is neatly situated below the kitchen counter, providing a good view for the family to watch while dinner's being prepared.

Credits: interior designer Linda Blair, ASID; photographer Kurt A. Dolnier

offices, where equipment not only is expected but adds to overall ambiance, set up differently than living rooms, which respond to many needs, some completely nonelectronic. Conversation, reading, family get-togethers, and company entertaining may or *may not* involve listening to music or watching television. Here, you want technology to be available but not to take command.

I'm always amused when I leaf through typical interior decoration and design books—oversized coffee-table volumes with photos of magnificently appointed, perfectly arranged rooms. Terribly misleading, I find, in many instances.

Missing from the photos and accompanying narratives are common-sense explanations of how you light these rooms without showing the wiring, how you can watch television or films on a rear screen projector without a heavy-duty cable in sight, or how a sleek, computer opened invitingly on a round, away-from-the-wall game table hooks up to its power source.

It's fashionable in theatrical design today to see the behind-the-scenes "works"—the overhead lighting and revolving stages. Your living room is not a theater, however, and living with the works at home can be messy and uninviting rather than dramatic.

Muted tones surround a large television screen; here's a media room featuring technological drama in a cleverly crafted environment.

Credits: interior designer Rosalyn Cama, ASID; photographer Tim Lee

BEHIND THE SCENES

- Hiding the wiring is not terribly difficult. Simply drop the cords from wall-mounted fixtures behind the walls. Two in-and-out holes will do the job, and a teaspoon or so of spackle can patch them up if you decide to move things around later.
- Floor cords can be buried beneath, again with two small in-and-out holes that connect equipment to electrical power. Wood-fill, available in your local hardware store, makes an excellent, virtually undetectable patch.
- To get under carpeting, try to separate the weave and work the cord through the small opening. You can manipulate the fibers back into place whenever you decide to withdraw the cord.

HOW SMART IS YOUR HOUSE?

The so-called smart house runs on a timer. Everything is calculated and calibrated to start and stop, speed up, and slow down automatically, with overrides programmed to interrupt and resume service to handle any contingency.

You would be wise to consult a professional designer before embarking on an elaborate high-tech plan. The permutations and combinations of units are vast, complicated, and, in spite of an advantageous size-to-capability ratio, space hogging. To preserve the homey atmosphere of your home—to keep it from looking more like an electronics showroom than family quarters—get professional help.

I am reminded of the quiet, elderly couple whose well-meaning children had installed in their parents' home an elaborate security system, kitchen-of-tomorrow appliances, computerized on–off outdoor lighting, and a music/TV system operated with a universal remote control. This, they figured would keep their parents safe and secure while they enjoyed excellent cuisine with little fuss and could while away many happy hours enjoying their favorite programs and concerts from the comfort of their easy chairs. Generous, high-tech children with low-tech parents.

The result: The couple became prisoners in their own home, afraid to venture outside lest they set off the alarm system—an action that in the past had summoned two police cars to their house with lights flashing and sirens blaring.

Their state-of-the-art kitchen appliances so complicated meal preparation that the couple began to rely more and more on frozen, prepared foods, even though they had enjoyed fixing fresh, simple meals for themselves.

The outdoor lighting, triggered by time or movement, blinked on and off during the night, often keeping them awake.

The remote control was so high-tech they couldn't find their favorite TV programs, so they watched whatever came on. Music was a thing of the past. They could load the CD player, but then couldn't get the thing to play.

Bottom line on technology: Let it serve you; don't be its slave. Integration without interference is the challenge today's designers are meeting.

*B*lairstyle *Tips*
on Creating a Workable Home Office

❖ You never can have too much money or too many closets, I say. And when it comes to electronics and technology, add to that list outlets and counter space.

❖ Think of your work area in terms of an L-shape or triangle—a niche that puts everything you'll need at arm's length, accessible with a swivel chair.

❖ Build in plenty of storage—lateral files for flat items, like blueprints and plans, and vertical cabinets with cubbies and slideout shelves for equipment and bulky items. Choose good quality metal cabinets that won't sag out of line.

❖ Project for 25 percent more space than current requirements dictate. That way you can grow your business without outgrowing your space.

❖ Plan for good lighting, overhead and general, as well as at least two task lights.

❖ For conferencing in a small area, choose a round table for softness and functional chairs that will swivel, pull up, and work anyplace in the room. Office chairs are among your most important purchases, because you tend to sit for long periods at a time. Consider a chair's comfort, durability, and support before its aesthetics.

❖ Tie the room together with woodwork and molding, corkboard backsplashes, and a tasteful blending of muted earth-tone colors and textured materials for floors, windows, and walls. This is your work place. You've got to feel good about the space.

12
ACCESSORIES
AND
DISPLAY

Liberate the Lonely Object; Celebrate the Whimsical; Rejoice in the Lopsided Beauty of the Unexpected

NO MATTER HOW beautifully your home is furnished, it's the accessories that reveal you—your unique personality, your character, your taste and judgment.

For a good part of my life, I've been involved with, concerned about, and surrounded by wonderful things. I like to liberate the lonely object, celebrate the whimsical, and rejoice in the lopsided beauty of the unexpected. I believe that, valuable or not, judiciously placed accessory objects contribute needed elements of the unexpected to every home.

Accessories tell a story. Unusual pieces resting on tables and window sills and adorning walls give status to everyday furniture. Accessories tell about faraway cultures and life in years gone by—many of these items so beautifully wrought, suggesting such interesting tales.

The craftsman's creation resting in a place of honor tells me as much about the collector as the artist. Even old aquamarine seltzer bottles with silver spigots lined up on a windowsill catch the light in amusing ways and reveal a sense of humor, the intimate truth about who lives there.

WHAT TO COLLECT; WHAT TO DISPLAY

You can display almost anything. I like to mix objects, amass collections, create vignettes. It's a question of relationships, textures, and proportions.

This is the point when a collection moves beyond random articles and becomes interior design. Display your cherished possessions to best advantage—in a group. A single item on each of the four corners of a table is an arrangement that forsakes connection, association, proximity, and impact.

Sometimes preferences seem idiosyncratic, having nothing to do with your perception of someone you feel you know very well. Other times they are a giveaway. "Of course," you say. "I might have known."

It came as no surprise to me that over the years one of my writer friends has amassed an extraordinary collection of books about words—reference tomes, dictionaries, grammar texts, advice and how-tos, humor books, works about writing by writers—a supportive addition to her obsession as well as her home.

A television producer, on the other hand, collects carvings of owls for his den. Why owls? Why not! Yet another collects tin soldiers, all sizes of figurines in wood, glass, clay, ivory, paper, and acrylic that seem to march across the coffee table.

Not surprisingly, a gifted kindergarten teacher made it a lifelong pursuit to collect Beatrix Potter books and dolls, which delighted generations of youngsters; another teacher chose Raggedy Ann dolls—not for her students but for herself—dozens of them arranged in a corner of her bedroom.

These collections are things that bring their owners pleasure, reflect their individuality, and inject personality into their living spaces.

Collecting is one of life's innocent pursuits—a safe, low-risk, intriguing way to pass the time. Displayed in your home, in a little nook or corner, or prominently in a handsome curio cabinet, accessories furnish the magic.

*Soft colors and soft
furnishings invite
relaxation.*
Credits: interior designer
Teri Seidman, Allied
Member ASID; photogra-
pher Bill Rothschild

*Upholstered seating
humanizes the dramatic
architectural detail in this
room, while colorful
accents add strength to the
seating area.*
Credits: interior designer
Carol Ann Maughn;
photographer Tim Lee

One rich, simple color on upholstered pieces, windows, and walls breathes softness.

Credits: interior designer Anthony Antine; photographer Bill Rothschild

Mixing types of seating adds unique charm to a typical dining setting. The Sheraton-style sideboard and built-in corner cabinet ensure ample serving and storage capabilities.

Credits: interior designer Michael A. Orsini, ASID; photographer Bill Rothschild.

One tall, important antique piece makes an entire room speak.

Credits: *Top left:* interior designer Anthony Antine; photographer Bill Rothschild
         Top right: interior designer Linda Blair, ASID; photographer Simon Cherry
         Bottom left: interior designer Teri Seidman, Allied Member ASID; photographer Bill Rothschild
         Bottom right: interior designer Albert E. Pensis; photographer Bill Rothschild

Take a plain wall and add designer ingenuity. The result: cabinets connected with a valance and curtains and a single bed, creating a charming and effective alcove out of empty space.
Credits: interior designer Nancy Mullan, ASID; photographer Bill Rothschild

Good design demands aesthetic appeal as well as good function. In these rooms custom storage says as much inside as it does outside.

Loft space requires more planning than other spaces; here a divider anchors a kitchen on one side and a bar on the other—another example of well-designed proportions and skilled execution.
Credits: interior designer Maggie Cohen, ASID; photographer Bill Rothschild

(Above, left)
Keeping cabinets, windows, and flooring the same wood provides a timeless serenity. Dark accents— granite backsplash, counter, chair seats, and a large painting—permit high contrast and drama
Credits: interior designer Allyn Kandel; photographer Bill Rothschild

(Above, right)
Frosted-glass doors on upper cabinets add a sense of openness, keeping the upper part of this galley kitchen from feeling claustrophobic.
Credits: interior designer Gail Shields-Miller; photographer Bill Rothschild

(Opposite)
Always classic, blue and white add character and punch to a white kitchen; note that the counters and island do not need to match.
Credits: interior designer Monte Berkoff; photographer Bill Rothschild

Old-fashioned charm often accounts for more than high tech; here three bathrooms that ignore the lure of renovation, opting instead to keep the old tiles and add precious accessories for fatal attraction.

Credits: *Left:* interior designer Sarah Boyer Jenkins, ASID; photographer Gordon Beall
          Center: interior designer Happy Martin; photographer Tim Lee
          Right: interior designer Teri Seidman, Allied Member ASID; photographer Bill Rothschild

Bathrooms have become the ultimate sybaritic experience. Traditional yet always fresh, white marble tiles on floors, walls, and tub surround create glamour without the cost of a slab installation.
Credits: interior designer Susan Mellis, Allied Member ASID; photographer Bill Rothschild

This space permits you to choose between watching a glowing fireplace, listening to music, watching entertainment or talking to friends—and offers spectacular light wood cabinetry as well.

Credits: interior designer Denise Balassi; photographer Bill Rothschild

No fireplace here, but the opportunity offered is to be together while doing different activities. Note the wood mixed with light cabinetry and upholstery.

Credits: interior designer Martin Kuckly; photographer Bill Rothschild

"More is more" when it comes to collections. Whether massing heirloom export china or antique botanical prints, the impact is strong when more than a dozen are present.

Credits: *Left:* interior designer Pat Sayers; photographer Bill Rothschild

        Right: interior designers Josef Pricci and Eaton Square Antiques; photographer Bill Rothschild

A pair of antique urns, flanked by portiere draperies, set the stage for a room full of unusual collectibles. But perhaps the best accessory is a vase of fresh tulips.

Credits: interior designer Charles J. Grebmeier; photographer Eric A. Zepeda

Antique accessories on a table skirted with Scalamandré fabric make a highly personal grouping.

Courtesy of Scalamandré

THE AURA OF THE OLD

What to collect? Consider this: "Antiques are the tangible heritage from our forefathers," declares Alice Winchester in her 1922 publication, *Living with Antiques*. "They are the useful and ornamental articles that our grandparents and our great grandparents created, lived with and loved . . . they give a home individuality and distinction. And in the world of change, they give evidence of stability and permanence."

The design on the vases echoes the upholstery pattern for double impact.

Credits: interior designer Joseph Braswell, ASID; photographer Ernst Beadle

A loose interpretation of the word *antique* gives wide berth. Turn me loose in a closet, let me rummage in an attic. . . .

Fabulous collections have been built from silver spoons, napkin rings, thimbles, kitchen tools, clocks and watches, buttons, military decorations, mechanical banks, cameras, dolls, photos, writing instruments, plates, glass bottles, walking sticks, chess sets, footstools, tea caddies, snuff boxes, bells, music boxes, musical instruments, theater programs, and match-books, among others. My client's beautiful paperweight collection began years ago with her search for the "perfect" gift for a friend.

I want you to become a collector, and I want you to start this minute. Begin by thinking about interesting items, noticing things, seeing objects—maybe for the first time. As a veteran of childhood wanderings with two generations of interior designers and antique dealers—my mother and her mother—I learned early on to recognize beauty in everything.

Use accessories as a room's focal point. The far wall of this dining room comes alive with a mirror, sconces, and a painting installed directly on the mirror

Credits: interior designer Linda Blair, ASID; renderer Robert So

How many is a collection? Less is less, I say. If one or two are good, ten are better. Learning will hone your editing skills. In time, as you go along, you'll know which ten are truly worthy keepsakes and which should be passed up or cast off.

But don't collect solely to decorate your home. Collect for the fun of collecting. Display becomes an enjoyable by-product, and your home the beneficiary.

FEAR NOT CLUTTER

To some, accessories are just things—clutter, dust collectors. Why, I wonder, are people hesitant about displaying articles meaningful to them? Is this the result of a too-much-of-a-good-thing neurosis? A minimalist mentality?

Unrelenting bareness is barren. Textureless space is trying. Every room, no matter how simply conceived, must introduce an element of tension. You've got to get something going somewhere. Even the most fierce anti-clutterists understand this concept.

The single rose, three bound books, one piece of art. Well chosen and well placed, in balance and proportion to its setting, each conveys and communicates. Accessories empower rooms.

Should you develop a serious case of ACD (Acquiring, Collecting, and Displaying)—which I sincerely hope you will—enjoy the hunt and relish the trophy. Your home will be all the better for your obsession.

A preliminary drawing shows background for a pottery and book collection that, when installed, will add warmth and intimacy to the massive stone wall.

Credits: interior designer Linda Blair, ASID; renderer Robert So

COLLECTING AND DISPLAYING ROOM BY ROOM

❖ *In the entry hall,* display photographs. An entry provides a doorway to the residence and photographs, framed on a small table or grouped on a wall, introduce its occupants. "Welcome to our home," the photos say.

A stairway to the upper floors is a natural art gallery site. Choose an eclectic mix of paintings and photographs in many sizes. For best results, mat and frame them and let them work their way up the staircase wall, illuminated by accent lighting and wall sconces.

Carve bookcases out of the wall to house books and accessories.

Credit: interior designer and renderer Robert So, Allied Member ASID

ENTRANCE FOYER

ROBERT SO DESIGNS

An entrance is a perfect place to hang a fabulous piece of art, setting the tone for the entire home.

Credit: interior designer and renderer Robert So, Allied Member ASID

❖ *In the living room and den,* display your collections—colorful fishing flies, ships encased in bottles, or bibelots—grouped on corner tables, in curio cabinets, or on an étagère.

❖ *In the family room or library,* enliven bookcases with groups of collectibles. As much as I love books, I need something to break up the horizontal line—a hint of the unexpected.

Old musical instruments are particularly well suited. A mandolin with its pear-shaped body, a recorder, a miniature piano, all manner of horns—lots of wood, strings, and brass. Display them on, under and next to the shelving for two great collections, books and music, happily commingled.

❖ *In the dining room,* mount your plate collection, or a series of posters, paintings, or photographs on the subject of food. Fewer is better here so

Accessories need to be personal and dramatic. Stacked plates in an open cupboard and a giant lemon painting give character to a country dining room.

Credits: interior designer Joseph Braswell, ASID; photographer Ernst Beadle

that the art doesn't compete with the people for attention. The focal point in the dining room should be the table—what's on it and who's around it. The dining room should stimulate conversation, not overpower it.

Aim for symmetry—five or six small pieces, matted and framed exactly alike, and hung along one wall approximately 15 inches above the chair rail.

❖ *In the bedroom,* create a quiet retreat. Identify a place for books and magazines, or surely they'll begin to pile up on the nightstands, a bedroom desk, or the floor.

Then invigorate the shelves with single objects you and your partner have found together on Saturday excursions or vacations—objects that recall adventures, funny experiences, intimate moments that solidify

Accessories can be anywhere—on top of the shutters and one the floor below the window seat.

Credits: interior designer Linda Blair, ASID; photographer Peter Krupeny

your relationship, objects that make you smile: a beautiful shell that washed up on the beach after a big storm, a silly statue you both found at a flea market and believed possessed magical powers.

❖ *In the guest room,* provide entertainment. Reading material, to be sure. People tend to travel with quick-read paperback books because they pack easily, but in fact they probably would rather read something more substantive.

War and Peace might be expecting too much of a weary guest, but a variety of current magazines and a collection of old ones spark the imagination. A collection of small windup toys that work adds charm and diversion.

❖ *In children's rooms,* resist a museum approach. Miniature china tea sets, antique dolls, and look-but-don't-touch dollhouses are noteworthy collectibles, but not for children. Don't litter children's rooms with them. They may look sweet to your friends, but they'll be a troublesome temptation to children forbidden to play with them.

Stick with the rough and tumble: stuffed animals, sturdy books, solid doll furniture, abuse-absorbing trucks and trains. You can display some on shelves or dresser tops, but be prepared to find them tossed into the all-purpose toy box, too.

The trick is to get children into collecting at a young age. Help them focus on a theme, and encourage the pursuit. Then display their collections, not yours.

❖ *In the kitchen,* work space is king. Cluttering valuable counter space with your collectibles seems impractical. Hang them instead—old kitchen tools on walls, unusual kitchen implements in iron or brass from ceiling hooks, strategically placed in out-of-the-way-yet-reachable spots.

Copper displays require polishing from time to time, but add warmth to kitchen walls. A series of copper frying pans hanging on a wall in the breakfast area brings three-dimensional interest, color, and theme to humble space.

❖ *In the bathroom,* decorate with a collection of plants, which will respond beautifully to steam. Create a bay window, fill it with colorful varieties, and watch them thrive. The worst brown thumb can cultivate lively plants in the bathroom.

*B*lairstyle Tips
on Displaying Accessories

❖ Make an impact by grouping objects. Don't scatter. Place similar shapes in groups of at least three or more. Raise some items slightly on stands or on books turned on their sides. Use height in all groupings. In addition to books and stands, I like obelisks and candlesticks.

❖ Group unique or humble things, like candlesticks or two or three pitchers, together. Put one on a stand, and turn the handles to face the same way. Create contrast in size, height, or color; closely placed items will show off each one's best assets. Group in uneven numbers, like three or five.

❖ Relate figures to each other; for a charming effect, keep turning them until they seem to talk to each other.

❖ Accessorize bookcases. Break up the unrelieved monotony of books, books, books with china or brass. Repeat the same items—like boxes—for eye-catching appeal. Turn some books on their sides. Rest one at an angle. Stagger plates at varying heights for punctuation.

❖ Choose tables, chests, tops of armoires, counters, floors, and even walls as surfaces to display accessories. Hang a collection of plates for instant charm. To add depth, mix in an occasional bracket topped by a vase or plate.

❖ Consider vases and flowers as accessories. Perhaps natural things are the most beautiful accessories of all.

*B*lairstyle Tips
for Mounting Artwork

❖ Position art on the walls in relation to other elements in the room—furniture, windows, ceiling height, and wall moldings. Before you begin hammering picture hooks into your walls, make a scale drawing and sketch in the pieces you want to hang.

❖ A large, important piece of art can stand alone; group smaller pieces together. Line up bottoms of pictures wherever possible.

❖ Position art at eye level. True, eye level varies quite a bit, but a range of five to six feet from the floor is about right, and quite forgiving. Keep in mind that in most instances lower rather than higher is the way to go.

❖ A high ceiling, on the other hand, calls for higher positioning on the walls to draw the eye upward and pull down the ceiling. The opposite is true of a low ceiling, where a vertical scheme will also appear to lift the ceiling.

❖ When grouping art, position the individual works close together. Wide separations interrupt continuity.

❖ Small pieces gain in importance with large mats. Mat with neutral colors—off-white and gray tones. Colored mats compete with the art.

❖ Mat photographs, posters, and watercolors.

❖ Keep artwork out of direct sunlight. Illuminate with wall washers and ceiling-mounted accent lights on tracks.

13
ERGONOMICS AND UNIVERSAL DESIGN

The art of interior design encompasses a vast number of details, not the least of which is comfort. Space that looks great, feels right and functions well satisfies real people in real-life settings.

—BETTY JO PURVIS, ASID
CHICAGO

Like Clothing, Furnishings Look and Feel Better If They Fit Well

FURNISHINGS AND CLOTHING have much in common. Both look and feel better when they fit well.

Maybe the fit of furnishings is a new idea to you. Clothing, as we all know, comes in petite, regular, and large sizes. As a subset within those categories, you can find short, regular, and long lengths, all of which can be mixed and matched.

Furnishings, however, come in one size. Unlike a navy blazer, say, which is available in many sizes to fit different body shapes, the navy couch you admire in the furniture store comes one way. You won't find it with a taller back and shorter seat cushions, or with firmer or softer filling. What you see is what you get. Either it fits or it doesn't.

Unfortunately, most people choose furnishings for looks alone. I hope that after reading the furniture chapters in this book, you will seek good construction as well. Keep in mind, though, you can find a good-looking sofa that's also good quality, but if it doesn't fit right, it's still not good for you.

This concept is called *ergonomics*—the applied science of furniture and equipment design intended to maximize productivity by reducing fatigue and discomfort. In simple terms, ergonomics refers to selecting furnishings for comfort and health as well as aesthetics.

ERGONOMICS AND INTERIOR DESIGN

The study of ergonomics excited me tremendously when I attended interior design school, and it still does. It is truly a great passion of mine. I care about my clients' comfort and physical health—whether their backs are supported and whether they get a good night's sleep.

In the New York metropolitan area, the television commercial tag line for the Syms discount clothing store, "An educated consumer is our best customer," is very well known. That's not only a brilliant advertising and marketing strategy, it's also absolutely true. The more you know, the more you know what to look for, and the more you appreciate it when you find it.

If you know how a quality sofa is put together and what elements identify a quality piece, you will become a more confident buyer.

Even though many home furnishings are subject to standard measurements, you can still find items that relate better than others to your own sense of comfort and proportion. Tune into how your body feels.

Ergonomics in the Workplace: Some Jobs Can Be a Real Pain

ERGONOMICS IN THE WORKPLACE is drawing national attention because workers are discovering that doing their jobs can be a real pain—in the neck, back, wrists, and pocketbook. As on-the-job injuries, worker's compensation claims, and the costs associated with lost work days skyrocket, ergonomics is taking center stage.

Too, with so many people working at home and spending long hours in front of computers, occupational hazards are as real in the home office as in the outside workplace. Manufacturers finally are addressing the problem and producing user-friendly office furnishings, from chairs with lumbar support to split computer keyboards.

The two most common on-the-job ailments are lower back pain and cumulative trauma.

In a basement home office, the most ergonomically comfortable chairs were selected for use both at the desks and at the conference table. Protecting and supporting backs is a good investment.

Credits: interior designer Linda Blair, ASID; photographer Arey Photography

HEALTHY DESIGN

Because the lower back bears a lot of weight and slips easily out of alignment, it is vulnerable to injury. To maintain a healthy back while working, position your chair and desk so that your feet touch the floor, your lower back is supported, and your upper back and neck are in a

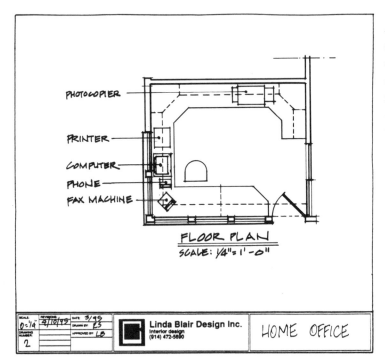

PHOTOCOPIER

PRINTER

COMPUTER

PHONE

FAX MACHINE

FLOOR PLAN
SCALE: 1/4" = 1'-0"

Linda Blair Design Inc.
Interior design
(914) 472-5690

HOME OFFICE

In a 12½-foot by 12-foot space, the comfort of easy-to-access storage and counter and an adjustable chair for long hours at the computer—all at a fingertip's reach.

Credits: interior designer Linda Blair, ASID; renderer Robert So.

LINDA BLAIR DESIGN INC.
Interior Design
(914) 472-5690
1 Chase Road, Scarsdale, N.Y. 10583

forward, neutral position. Your arms should rest comfortably at your side.

Cumulative trauma injuries occur when muscles and tendons are used repetitively for long periods. Carpal tunnel syndrome is one of the most common of these injuries; it is caused when muscles, tendons, or bones put pressure on the median nerve in the wrist.

As a designer, I care about the health and comfort of workers, whether they work at home or in the outside workplace, whether they're clients or not. An appropriate desk/chair/body relationship is important, along with frequent breaks, stretching, good posture and proper body mechanics, for good health on the job.

B *lairstyle Tips* *for Achieving Good Ergonomic Design at Home*

❖ If your back hurts or your legs feel tingly after sitting a while, the sofa doesn't fit. The trend toward overlarge, overstuffed furniture is a health hazard for short people. Low-slung furniture is equally poor for the tall or elderly. For best results, seek out firm seating with good back support.

❖ I always include several straight-backed chairs in every living room. Many adults prefer them to cushy pieces that tend to envelop. Slouching sounds better than it really is, particularly when it comes time to stand up. Gently lifting the body from a firm base to a standing position is far superior to a leapfrogging or hoisting approach.

❖ If you wake up in the morning feeling great—rested and relaxed— you've got a good mattress. If your neck, shoulders, and back ache, your mattress is sending you a message that your body is not being properly cushioned. To ensure even wear and body support, rotate the mattress twice a year—head to toe and side to side—and replace it every dozen or so years; consider the changes in your own body every 12 years or so.

Blairstyle Tips
for Achieving Good Ergonomic Design in the Workplace

❖ Desk height, chair height, and counter height all affect comfort, health, and productivity. Adjustability is the path to good ergonomics.

❖ Standard desk height varies from 26 to 30 inches; chair seat height, from 18 to 20 inches. Seek an ergonomically correct relationship by adjusting the height of the seat so that thighs are parallel to the floor and the backs of the knees are at a 90-degree angle.

❖ To minimize repetitive stress, such as carpal tunnel syndrome, position desk surface and chair height so that elbows are at a 90-degree angle when typing.

❖ When working at a computer, position the monitor about 18 to 20 inches from the eyes to reduce eye strain.

❖ Low and indirect ambient room light from a ceiling fixture or torch lamp, supported by task lighting over the desk, reduces glare.

❖ Maintain a pleasant mood with neutral colors. Bright colors can be intrusive, dark ones depressing.

❖ Maintain a comfortable temperature range, typically 68 to 72 degrees, and a humidity level at 30 to 40 percent. Low humidity is chilling; high humidity is enervating.

Universal Design Improves Living Conditions in Any Home

MARY E., A WHEELCHAIR-BOUND ATTORNEY, travels to work on a commuter railroad line, which designates the first space in every car for wheelchairs. She navigates busy city intersections via curb cuts, and enters her office building using the ramp access. She rides the elevator to the 18th floor and wheels herself into her office, which is equipped with a wide-access doorway that accommodates her chair. Her office is located just down a wide hall from the restroom, which has wheelchair-accessible light switches, sinks, and private commodes.

Mary's mobility and her office design have been made possible by the federal Americans with Disabilities Act (ADA) and an enhanced sensitivity to the needs of disabled Americans. The same provisions can be carried into the home to make life better and more comfortable for the disabled.

REWARDING EXPERIENCE

One of my first assignments as a consultant to the Easter Seal Society was to design and build a home wing for a wheelchair-bound and extremely bright youngster, whose parents wanted him to be able to function as comfortably and independently as possible at home. A quadriplegic, he could move only his mouth on a breathing tube.

I incorporated into the wing many barrier-free principles and other accommodations for his breather and access to his computer. In the end, I am very proud to say, we achieved an environment that provided this young boy with ample mobility for his comfort, health, self-confidence, and happiness.

UNIVERSAL DESIGN
FOR UNIVERSAL APPLICATION

Universal design is just that—universal. The applications are appropriate and helpful in any home.

In my own home, for instance, I installed a vertical handrail in the shower to prevent falls, and I have included barrier-free code-compliant 32-inch doorways in the plans for my new kitchen. I foresee lots of people in-and-out activity, and I want to be sure there's plenty of room.

Other barrier-free principles you can incorporate in your home include easy-to-use levers for door knobs and faucets, front-only stove burners, low placement of light switches on the walls, and a raised vanity height in the bathrooms. Most people, disabled or not, would benefit from these changes.

Barrier-free, or universal, design, like all good design, does not necessarily cost more. A door lever costs about the same as a knob, and a 32-inch doorway is actually cheaper to install than a regulation 29-inch because a wider door costs less than wall-making materials and is less labor intensive to install. From the point of view of interior design, a wide doorway provides drama and adds presence. For universal design, it permits everyone to enter.

A master bedroom and bath on the first floor are highly recommended for the not-so-young. Let the young relatives climb the stairs to the upstairs bedrooms.

And, in the final analysis, it's always cheaper to build it right the first time. If you don't need some of these conveniences right now, you may in the future. Be prepared. As I see it, barrier-free design has universal appeal.

If you were to see a totally barrier-free room model, my guess is that you wouldn't be aware of the changes. True, some of the proportions would be slightly different, but as long as they were in balance, the differences would be acceptable.

*B*lairstyle Tips on Incorporating Universal or Barrier-free Design Principles

❖ Replace door knobs and faucets with levers.

❖ Select a stove with burners and controls in the front.

❖ Reposition light switches lower on walls so that they are wheelchair accessible.

❖ Raise bathroom vanities to kitchen sink height.

❖ Lower bathroom mirrors for wheelchair accessibility.

❖ Install vertical handrails in showers and horizontal handrails in other rooms and along hallways and stairways.

❖ Create wide doorway openings.

❖ Study traffic patterns for optimal mobility.

❖ Build in plenty of storage to avoid clutter and prevent accidental falls.

14

WEAR AND TEAR AND MAINTENANCE

Nothing lasts forever. But good quality products diligently maintained will last longer. Maintenance is a little education and a lot of common sense.

—JOHN KELLY, ASID
PHILADELPHIA

The First Lesson of Good Design: Learn the Difference between Well-worn and Shabby

FAMILIAR SURROUNDINGS FEEL so comfortable. When you arrive home, weary from the trials of the day, the simple act of putting the key in the front door seems to relieve tension.

As you turn the opener in the latch, eager to get inside, you picture your welcoming front hall with its beautiful marbletop occasional table and antique mirror above. From the hallway, you'll be able to see the Oriental rug on the living room floor, and just for an instant you may remember how you agonized over the cost, never for an instant regretting your purchase.

You picture your favorite chair in the den, see yourself curled up with an afghan, watching a good movie. You can almost smell dinner heating in the oven, your kitchen table bidding you to sit with a cup of tea and the newspaper for a few minutes before the family bursts through the door.

Believe me, I know. When the day gets rough, images of home creep into my head, reminding me that there is light at the end of the day-long tunnel. Good design and lasting, quality purchases for your home create this oasis, this hideaway, this retreat that nourishes your spirit.

YOU LOOK BUT YOU DON'T SEE

The danger is that your home can become so familiar, so comfortable, that you fail to see the frayed edges, the nicks and scuffs, the dulled finishes, the chips and cracks, the withered leaves on the philodendron.

Is the marble on the hall table dulled from use? Has the wrought-iron frame on the antique mirror oxidized? Has dirt marred the vibrancy of the Oriental rug? Is the cushion on the den chair crushed flat? Is the upholstery soiled? Do the kitchen chairs need recaning? Should the oak table be refinished? Is the wallcovering stained? The paint discolored?

You look at this furniture, carpeting, paint, and wallpaper every day, but you don't see it. You're used to it, and it seems fine. Chances are, it's not.

You need to train yourself to look, to really see the condition of your home, your apartment, your office. If it's not up to snuff, you should do something about it, because one day, you're going to be away for an extended period—a month-long vacation, perhaps—and when you finally get back home, put the key into the latch, and picture the welcoming sights inside, you're going to be in for an unpleasant surprise. What you'll see is not what you imagined but what is real. And you'll be appalled.

And remember, no product is perfectly safe from nicks, scratches, or dirt.

A VIGOROUS ATTACK . . . INITIALLY

Not surprisingly, most interior design work is completed within 18 months of moving to a new location. Your new home, office, country retreat, or apartment beckons with possibilities—and imperfections. You make plans to repaint, wallpaper, redo the living room, update the kitchen. You replace windows, choose carpeting, buy furniture, and tear down walls to open up new, more serviceable living spaces.

You charge ahead, fired by your imagination and creativity, eager and determined to make your home comfortable, warm, pulled together, blemish-free—an absolute knockout, worthy of a spread in *Architectural Digest*.

And then you let it rest. And rest. And rest. You lose interest. The imperfections so glaring a few months ago meld into the whole. Meanwhile, you continue to live in your home, to cook and roast and spill and splatter in the kitchen, to shower daily, to drag dust and dirt across the carpets and floors, to sit on the chairs, to drop bundles against the baseboards.

You're not a careless person; in fact, you care a great deal about your possessions. Yet in the course of normal day-to-day living, signs of wear begin to appear. You've got to wake yourself up and make yourself see them. When it comes to your home, you need to hone your observation skills, to recognize the difference—the steep chasm—that separates well-worn from shabby. You've made an investment in the look of your home. Are you going to let that investment wither away? Where is the value in that?

REGULAR CLEANING IS NOT MAINTENANCE

Of course, you see that the furniture gets dusted, the pillows plumped, the carpeting vacuumed, and the kitchen and bathrooms washed down regularly. And you keep a tight rein on clutter—picking up, putting away, tossing out, storing, riding herd on the children.

A home needs more. Regular cleaning is not maintenance.

There are steps you can and should take to preserve your fine purchases and your decorating plan. No product can absorb heavy use and continue to look new. True, in many cases this is an advantage. Fine hardwoods, for instance, tend to improve with age, taking on a patina that makes them more beautiful and more lustrous than when new—if you oil the wood to keep it from drying out and cracking, or apply polish or wax from time to time to maintain the veneer.

Other materials do not hold up as well, however, and begin to show signs of age. As we know from reflections in our own mirrors, the indicators can be harsh and unattractive.

Regular body maintenance rewards the effort with supple skin and good health. The dividends of regular home maintenance include enduring beauty and comfort. In fact, with proper maintenance some home investments may actually increase in value. An Oriental rug, for instance, can serve for decades and sell for three times its original price.

Proper maintenance requires relatively little attention and time. You'll find that a little can accomplish a lot. The information that follows will help you preserve the look and the value of your possessions.

Wood Furniture

I love old wood, its surfaces etched with a patina of subtle shadings and layers of wear. My collection of honey-colored wooden tools and finials never fails to enchant me with its still-rich look after 100 years of use.

Wood furniture is perhaps the easiest surface to maintain. Dust, polish, or wax occasionally, and oil every five years or so if your house is particularly dry. That's really all that's needed.

Unlike other materials, antique wood finishes dulled and chipped by age and use often are more valuable and certainly are more interesting than when new. Painted wood finishes, for instance, their base colors peeking through, provide a delightful sense of history. Even a starkly modern setting responds well to an aged chair or bureau.

On the other hand, a rickety chair should be examined for loose dowels that may need regluing. Drawer pulls nearly pulled off from years of use should be reattached. No patina is rich enough to save these ill-maintained pieces.

Hardwood Floors

Hardwood floors will stay beautiful and last a lifetime with regular care and maintenance. In general, try to keep dirt, grit, and sand from settling on the floor; the particles act as an abrasive and dull the finish.

Vacuum regularly, with a brush attachment, as often as you vacuum carpets. Sweep or use a dust mop daily or as needed, but do not use a dust treatment, which can become slick or dull the finish.

Never damp mop a wax-finish wood floor unless polyurethane has been applied.

Wipe up food and other spills immediately, using a dampened—not wet—cloth if necessary. Then dry the area with another cloth or paper towel.

Women's high heels are a wood floor's worst enemy. A 125-pound woman wearing three-inch heels exerts a force of 2,000 psi (pounds per square inch) on a hardwood floor—that's more than an average car (28 to 30 psi) or an elephant (50 to 100 psi). Moreover, worn-down heels that have lost their protective cap will dent any floor surface, even concrete.

- To maintain the luster of a wax finish, buff every other month or so, depending on use, and wax only when absolutely necessary, typically no more than once or twice a year.

- To maintain a polyurethane finish, add a quarter-cup of white vinegar to a quart of warm water, and sponge on with a barely damp mop. Wipe dry with a towel as you go. Do not wax.

- White and bleached floors, like white carpet or vinyl, are more susceptible to the effects of dirt and traffic than floors with natural or dark stained finishes. As a result, they require more attention.

  Vacuum or sweep often, and follow the directions appropriate to the finish. Note that tiny separations may occur between floor strips during dry seasons or long heating periods, when low humidity levels cause wood to contract. The contrast of a white floor surface causes even tiny separations to appear larger, but rest assured that the situation is temporary, although annual. Also, white floors may show shading changes over time.

Hardwood Floor First Aid

Here are some first aid suggestions for common accidents on wax-finish floors:

- For dried milk or food stains, gently rub with a damp cloth.

- For stains caused by standing water, rub spot with triple-zero steel wool and rewax.

- To remove dark spots, ink, animal or diaper stains, clean spot and surrounding area with triple-zero or double-zero steel wool and a wood floor cleaner or odorless mineral spirits; wash with household vinegar; sand with fine-grain sandpaper; and stain, rewax, and polish.

- To remove marks from heels or casters, rub with fine steel wool dampened with your usual wax; buff to a shine.

- To remove mold, apply a good cleaning fluid.

- To remove chewing gum, crayon, or candle wax, apply ice until the deposit becomes brittle and crumbles off. Solvent-based wax poured around the area (not on it) will soak under the deposit and loosen it.

- To remove cigarette burns, rub with steel wool moistened with solvent-based wax.

- To remove oil and grease stains, rub on a kitchen soap with a high lye content, or saturate cotton with hydrogen peroxide and place it over the stain; then saturate a second layer of cotton with ammonia and place it over the first layer. Repeat until the stain is gone.

- To remove wax buildup, strip old wax with odorless mineral spirits and rub with fine steel wool; apply new wax.

Iron and Other Metals

Iron and metalwork stand up to use and abuse better than any other product and require little maintenance. Metalwork that is hammered, wrought, or stippled provides a welcome addition to rooms of every style.

Oxidation, a chemical reaction of metal when combined with oxygen, may cause some materials to rust. Iron is particularly apt to oxidize. Apply a rust inhibitor, available at hardware stores, or a rust remover if spots have begun to appear.

Marble and Stone

Although magnificent to look at and highly durable, marble, slate, and granite finishes will stain. However, these nonporous surfaces are also easy to maintain.

Clean with water, using a mild soap (like Ivory Liquid) if necessary. Perhaps every two years, depending on use, apply an acrylic, water-based sealer to bring back the shine. Never use abrasive products or strong chemicals.

Ceramic Tile

Easy maintenance is one of the major advantages of ceramic floor tile. Soap and water will take care of virtually any spill.

Be sure to keep a supply of about half a dozen spare tiles (from the installed dye lot) on hand in case of breakage. Ceramic tile is quite durable, but the clay can fracture if you drop something heavy on it. A professional installer can dig out a cracked tile, replace it, and regrout.

For bathroom applications, note that some wall grouts contain a fungicide that resists mold and mildew. Epoxy grouts create impervious, waterproof surfaces. Silicone rubber grout resists staining, moisture, mildew, cracking, and shrinking.

Decorative Laminates and Solid Surface Materials

Durability and easy maintenance make high-pressure decorative laminates and solid-surface materials excellent choices for countertops in kitchens and baths. Today's Formica and Corian surfaces, among other brands, come in a variety of patterns, many simulating more expensive materials like marble and granite.

To clean them, warm water and a mild detergent will do the trick, with no loss in finish. To remove stains, rub gently with medium or light sandpaper, or Scotch-Brite pads. Never use harsh chemicals, such as paint remover, turpentine, nail polish remover, or stove and drain cleansers.

Rugs and Carpeting

Your carpet will last longer and look better if you follow the three basic rules of carpet maintenance: vacuum regularly, remove spills immediately, and professionally clean, usually once a year.

Vacuum at least once a week, and more often in heavy traffic areas. This will remove soil and dirt particles before they become embedded in the pile.

An upright vacuum cleaner with a rotating beater bar, or a brush or canister type with a power head are the most efficient cleaners. For Berber-style carpets (coarse loop pile) use a suction-only vacuum cleaner to reduce fuzzing.

Move the vacuum cleaner slowly to allow time to get out all the dirt, and make sure the dust bag is never more than half full. You cannot overvacuum. Vacuuming should begin the day the carpet is installed.

For successful spot removal, blot (do not rub) spills with white paper towels or a clean, absorbent cloth. Scoop up solids with a knife or spoon.

Pretest spot-removal products in an inconspicuous area. Place a few drops of the cleaning agent on the carpet, and blot it after 10 minutes with a paper towel. If the color of the carpet changes, do not use this cleaning agent.

You can make an effective cleaning agent by mixing a teaspoon of clear dishwashing liquid or detergent powder with a cup of warm water. Or mix one tablespoon of clear household ammonia (3-percent solution) with a half-cup of water. Or mix a third-cup of white vinegar with two-thirds-cup of water.

Apply a cleaning agent (either home prepared as above or a dry cleaning solvent available at grocery, drug, and hardware stores) to an absorbent towel, not the carpet, and begin to blot up the spill. Do not over-wet the carpet. Work inward from the edge of the spot to prevent excessive spreading. Then rinse with clear warm water, working from the edge to the center. Do not rub. Finally, remove excessive moisture by applying pressure with paper towels or absorbent cloths.

When having your carpet professionally cleaned, use a reputable company and check references. Deep-cleaning and steam-extraction methods work best because they draw from the base of the carpeting and remove dirt that shifts to the bottom.

Wall-to-wall installations are cleaned on the premises. Typically, area rugs are picked up and cleaned off the premises. When ready, they are delivered and placed in position by the dry cleaner.

Fabrics

Textiles are the most fragile design products in your home. Sun, dirt, stains, and air pollutants exact a heavy toll.

In general, tightly woven tapestries, which are excellent choices for upholstery, stand up best and will look wonderful even after half a century of use. Loosely woven fabrics that let light pass through are better choices for window treatments, of course, but are less durable. Whatever fabrics you choose, proper maintenance will help them last longer.

As a rule, natural fibers wear better than synthetics, although the blends are somewhat easier to care for. Among the natural fibers:

- **Cotton** is strong, but will break down in sunlight. Appropriate for draperies and upholstery, cotton is machine washable but requires ironing.

- **Linen** is extremely strong, but wrinkles easily and can feel stiff to the touch. Because its texture tends to repel dirt, linen is a good drapery fabric, particularly if you like to open your windows. Professional dry-cleaning is advised.

- **Silk**, like cotton, will weaken in sunlight and will stain if splashed with water. Combined with other fabrics, however, it is highly durable with a graceful, elegant look. Dry-clean for best results.

- **Wool**, strong as well as versatile, is appropriate for upholstery and draperies. It resists the harmful effects of sunlight and will keep its shape longer than other natural fibers. Wool should be professionally dry-cleaned.

- **Synthetic fabrics** can be used alone or combined with other fibers for maximum advantage. Be aware, though, that depending on the blend, synthetic fabrics can take on a "synthetic look"—an abnormal sheen, a tendency to pill, or an unpleasant feel.

  Nevertheless, most synthetics mean easy care. For the most part, polyesters, nylons, and acrylics can be hand-washed. Rayon and acetate should be professionally dry-cleaned. All synthetics weaken in sunlight.

Fabric Finishes

- Fabric finishes applied at the mill add strength and longevity to fabrics, making them more resistant to normal household perils. Happily, these additives rarely alter a fabric's character or color, but have been developed to protect against such environmental hazards as fire, stains, soil, insects, mildew, molds, moths, and the like. Some finishes discourage wrinkling; others repel water.

- While natural fibers are naturally flame resistant, synthetics not only will burn but can melt. *A chemical treatment that resists fire ignition and retards the spread of flame offers considerable protection, but no application is fireproof.* Check the manufacturer's specifications for information about any fabrics you choose for your home.

- Carpeting and upholstery fabrics treated with a soil- or stain-re-sistant finish, or both at the factory lengthen fabric life. An anti-stain finish keeps spills "sitting on the top" of a fabric so you can easily wipe them away rather than allow the liquid to soak in. An anti-soiler keeps dirt and dust from permeating the fabric surface.

- If a drapery or upholstery fabric you have chosen doesn't come with a stain- or soil-resistant finish, you can have one applied to the merchandise at the factory. Or you can purchase a spray-on foam and apply it yourself. It's easy to use and works perfectly well.

- Stain and soil finishes *resist* spills and dirt, but do not *prevent* them, even with gentle use. Sooner or later, you will have to clean all fabric-based products of dust and dirt and normal wear and tear. For best results, consult a quality professional cleaner.

B lairstyle Tips for Home Maintenance

- **Attend to maintenance tasks on a regular basis to keep your home always inviting. If you need to undertake a major cleanup before guests arrive, you'll find yourself issuing invitations less frequently.**

- **By spreading out major house and household chores over 12 months, you will be able to do all of them without straining your time or your finances.**

- **Don't try to do everything yourself. Many house and household chores are best handled by professionals, whose fees can be** included in your monthly maintenance budget. A maintenance budget will preserve good design and provide good value, protecting your investments from deteriorating.

• Adapt the following home maintenance calendar to your situation, with the aid of reliable professional help.

*B*lairstyle *Home Maintenance Calendar*

❖ DAILY

  • Plump sofa and chair cushions.
  • Damp-mop entryway and kitchen floor.
  • Sweep outside entryway.

❖ WEEKLY

  • Usual cleaning.
  • Remove spots from furniture and floor covering.

❖ MONTHLY

  • Dust slats in blinds.
  • Vacuum dust from draperies.
  • Remove mildew buildup in bathrooms.
  • Clean ceiling fixtures and chandeliers.

❖ JANUARY

  • Create a house file. Include blueprints, plot plan, all appliance instruction books, insurance policies, and names of service people: heating/air conditioning service, plumber, electrician, window washer, gardener, chimney sweep, carpenter, mason, pool service.
  • Locate the fuse boxes and attach a diagram to each box indicating which fuse covers which rooms or appliances.
  • Locate the shutoff valve to each faucet and toilet and the main water cutoff valve.

- Locate the gas shutoff valve.
- Locate the restart button for the furnace.
- Learn how the fireplace works and how to build a good fire.
- Arrange for a fire inspection; install smoke detectors, and plan an emergency escape route.
- Arrange for a police security inspection; change all locks to operate with a single key, and hide one key outside.
- Make duplicate keys for house, cars, garage door opener, safe, file cabinets, storage shed, and the like; store in a secure place.
- Arrange for an annual termite inspection.
- Purchase a first aid kit, portable radio, flashlight and batteries, candles or kerosene lamp and fuel, scissors, string, matches, extension cords, and some basic tools (hammer, pliers, assorted nails, screws and bolts, saw, garden hose, outdoor broom, and Phillips and straight-blade screwdrivers).
- Examine kitchen and bathroom towels and all bedding; replace if necessary, taking advantage of January white sales.

❖ FEBRUARY

- Check the water level in the boiler weekly; flush excess.
- Check electric cords and wall receptacles; replace if necessary.
- Check the attic for damp spots that indicate leaks, seepage from roof gutters, or condensation.
- Shake heavy, wet snow off branches of trees and shrubs; weight can bruise branches.

❖ MARCH

- Tighten hinge screws in all doors; lubricate pins. Check to see that all doorknobs are functioning properly.
- Replace cracked windowpanes; cold causes windows to crack.
- Clean gutters and downspouts of debris.
- Look for loose flashing around chimneys, vent pipes, and dormers; replace missing shingles.
- Get garden tools ready; schedule gardener.
- Turn the mattresses.

❖ APRIL

- Replace batteries on doorbells, smoke detectors, burglar alarms, and intercom systems. (When you change your clocks, change your batteries.)
- Turn on water to outside faucets.
- Unplug holes in lawn sprinkler systems and clean rust with steel wool.
- Clean out basement and attic; accumulation is a fire hazard.
- Wash windows.
- Wash curtains.

❖ MAY

- Repair masonry—bricks, foundations, retaining walls, walkways, and driveways. Examine basement walls and floor for damp areas and repair if necessary.
- Put house plants outside.
- Test central air conditioning, or install individual window units; clean and oil the attic fan.
- Call the swimming pool service people.
- Repair window and door screens.
- Install awnings; replace worn pulleys and cords.
- Clean and set up patio, deck, and porch furniture.

❖ JUNE

- Check air conditioners periodically through the hot weather; clean filters when necessary, and lubricate to preserve energy efficiency.
- Clean out closets, drawers, and kitchen cabinets.

❖ JULY

- Inspect brick and stucco walls; repair crumbled mortar.
- Fill or patch depressions in blacktop surfaces.

❖ AUGUST

- Have the heating system serviced.

- Clean out the garage.
- Examine kitchen and bathroom towels and all bedding; replace if necessary, taking advantage of August white sales.
- Clean out kitchen cabinets; discard or replace old provisions.

❖ SEPTEMBER

- Caulk and weatherstrip around doors, windows, and foundation; proper sealing will prevent moisture damage in winter and keep you more comfortable.
- Check the south side of the house for signs of peeling paint caused by exposure to direct sun.
- Have a chimney sweep clean the fireplace and flue.
- Turn the mattresses.
- Remove books from exposed shelving and dust thoroughly.

❖ OCTOBER

- Reinforce or replace weakened fence portions.
- Replace screens with storm windows and doors.
- Remove air conditioners from windows, or cover them for the winter.
- Arrange for snow removal.
- Bring in house plants.
- Replace batteries on doorbells, smoke detectors, burglar alarms, and intercom systems. (When you change your clocks, change your batteries.)
- Have carpeting, draperies, and upholstered furniture professionally cleaned.
- Wash windows.
- Clean and put away patio, deck and porch furniture.

❖ NOVEMBER

- Clean gutters, downspouts, window wells, and flat roofs of debris.
- Clean shower heads—unscrew and remove sediment and mineral deposits with a brush. Likewise, kitchen sink spray unit and all faucets; change washers if leaks occur.

- Disconnect the lawn sprinkler assembly; turn off and drain outdoor faucets.
- Remove all items from china and curio cabinets and clean. No cabinet is airtight; dust will seep in.

❖ DECEMBER
- Replace leaking radiator valves.
- Vacuum condenser coils behind and underneath the refrigerator to increase efficiency.
- Be prepared for midwinter power failures; replace flashlight batteries, and check supply of candles, kerosene lamps, and fuel.
- Take a walking tour through every room of the house; make a list of remodeling, renovation, repair, and replacement projects for the new year. Look for chipped paint, furniture nicks, worn carpeting and upholstery, broken floor and wall tiles, and yellowing wallpaper.
- If you live in an apartment, call the super or handyman for some of the tasks listed above—one advantage to not owning a home.
- Enjoy a happy and secure holiday season.

15
FINAL
BLAIRSTYLE
TIPS

Recipe for design success: gently stir quality ingredients and fine workmanship into a well-conceived plan. Add personality and individuality. Season with taste. Serves well, and keeps for years and years.

—LINDA BLAIR, ASID
SCARSDALE

Be Prepared to Compromise, Not to Settle

WE HAVE COME nearly to the end of our first journey together in the fascinating sea of interior design. I hope you will be better prepared sailors for an actual interior design experience, more confident of your ability to chart your own course on the way to comfortable, stylish, and successful rooms.

I hope, too, that you will be more aware of the inherent value of quality materials and labor and their place in selecting merchandise and planning good design. Beware of bargains that are no bargains.

For example, a friend wanted to replace the six designer chairs in her kitchen, but found that the price had gone up dramatically since she first bought the chairs 14 years ago. I am happy to report that she heeded my buy-quality message. Rather than buying six new chairs of lesser quality, she bought four of the top-quality chairs at the higher price and recovered two of the originals.

She compromised, but she didn't settle. I think she made a smart choice. Good quality is good value.

MAKE POSITIVE DECISIONS

Along the same theme, my writer friend, whom I mentioned previously, discovered a marvelous, oversized, circa-1920 rolltop desk at an antique shop near her home. An equally oversized problem materialized at the time of delivery, however. The furniture movers simply couldn't get the thing through her office door. They took the door off its hinges, removed the moldings from the inside of the door jamb, and even unscrewed the rolltop from the desk top. Still, they couldn't get the piece into the room.

The dealer suggested she have the doorway or, better still, a window enlarged so that the piece could be hoisted in from the outside—both very expensive options that put the price of the desk out of reach.

My friend was devastated, her dream of writing the great American novel on an old rolltop desk shattered. She replaced the moldings, rehung the door, sent the desk back to the shop, and decided to settle for a new desk she had seen in a department store—one that would fit through the door.

The desk was quite handsome, actually, but it wasn't what she wanted. I convinced her to keep working on the kitchen table for a while longer and to continue her search, certain that in time she would find a desk to purchase for a positive reason, not a negative one.

She swears it was divine intervention—the answer to her prayers—that an ever-so-slightly smaller rolltop desk virtually reached out and grabbed her by the arm as she was window-shopping one Saturday afternoon. It had the same double-tiered bottom drawers on either side of an amply large kneehole opening as the first one, the same eight additional drawers, and the same 34 little cubbyholes; plus, it had two secret compartments—an intriguing and totally irresistible feature.

She bought it, and while she hasn't yet produced the great American novel, she is happy and more productive than ever before in her writing career.

Did she compromise? Yes. Did she settle? Not hardly.

SEEK PROFESSIONAL HELP

Let me reiterate, too, that a novice should never undertake complex design plans without professional help. What is a complex plan? Any plan that requires reconstruction or repositioning of architectural room elements, new plumbing or electrical work, the acquisition of art, or the purchase of costly accessories should be planned, coordinated, monitored, and overseen by a professional designer, who will guide you in making a wise investment and see to the satisfactory conclusion of the project.

A designer can help you balance priorities, apportion your design dollars, and guide you through that all-important planning stage with simple projects, too. A designer can suggest ways to maximize use of space, provide access to trade-only showrooms, and save you from making expensive mistakes.

Even if you want to do it yourself, a designer can help you choose colors and fabrics and suggest a furniture arrangement that will work for you.

If you've never worked with a designer, you can call the American Society of Interior Designers (ASID) referral service at (800) 775-ASID for the names of member designers in your area, or call your local ASID chapter.

SELECTING A DESIGNER

For best results, I highly recommend that you interview the designer about his or her work, as much as the designer will interview you in connection with the project you have in mind. Consider these factors in selecting a designer:

❖ *Enthusiasm for the project.* If the designer seems indifferent about, say, updating rather than redoing your kitchen, look elsewhere. A designer should bring creative energy to every project, regardless of the budget.

❖ *Receptivity to your ideas.* An interior designer works on your behalf—for you. You must feel comfortable trusting your designer's taste and judgment, yet the project must be yours and most certainly must reflect your personality and individuality.

❖ *Respect for your budget.* With any reasonable budget, an experienced designer can make any room better. True, he or she cannot develop a new state-of-the-art kitchen without a sizable investment on your part, but a modest investment can improve the existing kitchen. State your budget at the outset and ask the designer what can be accomplished with that figure. Agreement at the outset on design goals and costs will prevent unpleasant misunderstandings later.

❖ *Good references.* Referral and reputation are the best advertisements for any service business, particularly in the discipline of interior design, where new work in your home may temporarily disturb the running of the household. Putting in a new kitchen is probably the most unsettling of all design projects under the best of circumstances, even though a new kitchen provides one of the most satisfactory results. Hence, another person's good renovation experience bodes well for you and your project.

❖ *Acceptable fees.* Designers charge differently. Some charge a flat fee, others commission or retail, or hourly rates. Be sure you understand how your designer sets fees before you assign any work. A good designer will spell out the scope of services to be rendered and methods of compensation in writing before any work begins

Generally, designers are able to buy products at wholesale prices, and most will pass along the savings to their clients, charging them less than full retail.

Keep in mind, too, that through the years a designer builds up valuable contacts with custom workrooms and tradespeople who can perform quality installation work, and has sources for unusual products and services. This reference file is well worth the designer's fee for executing the project.

You must be familiar with the fee system and the billing process. Get it in writing before you begin.

AND, FINALLY . . .

And finally, have fun. Interior design is an endlessly fascinating expedition that offers formidable challenges as well as long-term rewards. Good luck and much success in your quest for good design and good value.

Special thanks to my ASID design colleagues around the nation whose words and work inspire me . . .

CHAPTER 1—MAKE A PLAN
Rita Carson Guest, ASID
Carson Guest, Inc.
Atlanta, Georgia

CHAPTER 2—WALLS AND CEILINGS
Gary E. Wheeler, FASID
The Wheeler Group
Minneapolis, Minnesota

CHAPTER 3—FLOORS
Jon J. Fields, FASID
Edward Fields Incorporated
New York, New York

CHAPTER 4—LIGHTING
Charles J. Grebmeier, ASID
Grebmeier & Associates, Inc.
San Francisco, California

CHAPTER 5—WINDOWS AND DOORS
Lloyd Bell, FASID
Lloyd Bell Associates
New York, New York

CHAPTER 6—FABRICS AND WINDOW
TREATMENTS
Barbara Schlattman, ASID
Barbara Schlattman Interiors
Houston, Texas

CHAPTER 7—COLOR AND PATTERN
Joseph P. Horan, ASID
Joseph Horan Interior Design
San Francisco, California

CHAPTER 8—SOFT FURNISHINGS
Robert Herring, IF-ASID
F. Schumacher & Co.
New York, New York

CHAPTER 9—HARD FURNITURE
John Elmo, FASID
Elmo Design Group, Ltd.
Yonkers, New York

CHAPTER 10—KITCHENS AND BATHS
Sarah Jenkins, ASID
Sarah Boyer Jenkins & Associates, Inc.
Chevy Chase, Maryland

CHAPTER 11—TECHNOLOGY
Rosalyn Cama, ASID
Rosalyn Cama Interior Design Associates, Inc.
New Haven, Connecticut

CHAPTER 12—ACCESSORIES AND DISPLAY
Joseph Braswell, ASID
Joseph Braswell & Associates
New York, New York

CHAPTER 13—ERGONOMICS AND
UNIVERSAL DESIGN
Betty Jo Purvis, ASID
PPM Design Associates
Chicago, Illinois

CHAPTER 14—WEAR AND TEAR AND
MAINTENANCE
John Kelly, ASID
John Kelly Interior Design
Philadelphia, Pennsylvania

My appreciation to the talented designers whose photographed work adds so much to this book:

Anthony Antine
Antine Associates, Fort Lee, New Jersey

Denise Balassi
Interior Consultants, South Salem, New York

Karen Berkemeyer
Ceramic Design, Greenwich, Connecticut

Monte Berkoff
Bisulk Kitchens, Garden City, New York

Joseph Braswell, ASID
Joseph Braswell & Associates, New York, New York

Nancy Brous
Eaton Square Antiques, Southampton, New York

Rosalyn Cama, ASID
*Rosalyn Cama Interior Design Associates, Inc.
New Haven, Connecticut*

Maggie Cohen, ASID
Room Service Designs, Inc., New York, New York

Rena Fortgang, Allied Member ASID
Locust Valley, New York

Stephanie Stephens Gans
New York, New York

Charles J. Grebmeier
Grebmeier & Associates, Inc., San Francisco, California

Joseph P. Horan, ASID
Joseph Horan Interior Design, San Francisco, California

Sarah Jenkins, ASID
Sarah Boyer Jenkins & Associates, Inc., Chevy Chase, Maryland

Allyn Kandel
Allyn Kandel Designs, Roslyn, New York

Cynthia Kasper, ASID
Interior Accents, Redding, Connecticut

Mary Knackstedt, ASID
Harrisburg, Pennsylvania

Diane Alpern Kovacs
Diane Alpern Kovacs Interior Design, Inc., Roslyn, New York

Martin Kuckly
Kuckly Associates, Inc., New York, New York

Vince Lattuca
Visconti & Co., New York, New York

Jeanne Leonard
Jeanne Leonard Interiors, Westhampton Beach, New York

Happy Martin
New York, New York

Carol Ann Maughn
Carol Ann Maughn Design, Scarsdale, New York

Susan Mellis, Allied Member ASID
Scarsdale, New York

Sandra Morgan, ASID
Sandra Morgan Interiors, Inc., Greenwich, Connecticut

Nancy Mullan, ASID
N. D. M Kitchens, Inc., New York, New York

Michael A. Orsini, ASID
Levithan/Orsini, Inc., New York, New York

Albert E. Pensis
Pensis-Stolz, New York, New York

Josef Pricci
New York, New York

Marilyn H. Rose
Marilyn H. Rose Interiors, Ltd., Locust Valley, New York

Pat Sayers
Design Resources of L.I., Inc., Huntington, New York

Edward and Adriana Scalamandré Bitter, ASID
Scalamandré, Long Island City, New York

Teri Seidman, Allied Member ASID
Teri Seidman Interiors, New York, New York

Gail Shields-Miller
Shields & Company Interiors, New York, New York

Barbara Schlattman, ASID
Barbara Schlattman Interiors, Inc., Houston, Texas

Robert So, Allied Member ASID
Robert So Designs, Fairfield, New Jersey

Joan Spiro, ASID
Joan Spiro Interiors, Great Neck, New York

Anne Tarasoff
Anne Tarasoff Interiors, Port Washington, New York

Miriam Wohlberg
Miriam Wohlberg Interiors, Merrick, New York

About the Author

LINDA BLAIR, a third-generation interior designer known for her keen sense of quality and taste, has built an award-winning, nationally known interior design firm. Her practice encompasses new installations and renovations of residential, commercial, and vacation properties. Harmony of design and design that creates a harmonious life are her paramount criteria.

Helping consumers make good design and buying decisions has been a major goal throughout Linda's career. This focus makes her a frequent choice not only as project designer but also as a radio/TV guest, lecturer, and writer.

Linda has appeared many times on the Lifetime Cable Television Network's "Our Home" show, and also has appeared on a "Weekend Today" showhouse tour with NBC's Al Roker. Her design ideas have been featured in *The New York Times, Cosmopolitan, The New York Daily News, Qualified Remodeler, Home Office Computing, Custom Home*, and the *ASID Report*, among others. Her column, "Blairstyle," appears often in the *New York Post*. Recent speaking engagements have included Lighting for the Elderly at New York's Jacob Javits Center, Code Compliance in Period Interiors for the Landmarks Commission/Brownstone Revival Committee, and New York Design Week's Spotlight on Kitchens. She has taught courses on building codes and interior design at Pace University, the Parsons School of Design, and the New York School of Interior Design.

A past president of the Metropolitan New York chapter of the American Society of Interior Designers, and a consultant to the National and New York Easter Seal Societies and the New York City Office on Disability, Linda is listed in *Who's Who of American Women & Women Executives* and *Who's Who of Interior Design*.

Linda and her husband, Bill Doescher, live in Scarsdale, New York, where she serves on the Board of Architectural Review, the Town and Village Civic Club's zoning and planning committee, and the advisory board of the Scarsdale Historical Society. The couple have four grown children.

INDEX